Unorthodox

For Jamie, patron saint of friendship

Unorthodox

LGBT+ Identity and Faith

Edited by Séan Richardson

Five Leaves Publications

Unorthodox: LGBT+ Identity and Faith
Edited by Séan Richardson

Published in 2019 by Five Leaves Publications
14a Long Row, Nottingham NG1 2DH
www.fiveleaves.co.uk
www.fiveleavesbookshop.co.uk

ISBN: 978-1-910170-60-1

Printed in Great Britain

Contents

Introduction *Séan Richardson*   7

Leap of Faith *Rachel Mann*   11

Our Own Histories *Maryam Din*   25

Dance is My Devotion *Jaivant Patel*   35

In My DNA *Isabella Segal*   43

The Things I Can't Put Into Words *Sabah Choudrey*   51

Path of Many Journeys *Selina Khunkhuna*   59

No Man's Land *Mr Ekow*   67

The Worm in the Hand *Siddhi Joshi*   75

Everything in Context *Khakan Qureshi*   81

My Faith is My Nani *Daljinder Johal*   89

Conversation Across a Table *Ben and Robert*   97

Holy Books *Mark Solomon*   109

Contributors   121

Acknowledgements   124

Introduction

Séan Richardson

As a queer person from an Irish Catholic family, three things were destined to be an inescapable part of my life: food, guilt, and mothering. Food is my love language. Cooking for partners and friends is how I show that I care. When those around me are down or anxious or in the mood to celebrate, I turn first to a pan of roast potatoes, gold at the centre and edged with fine brown cracks. Guilt is the permanent condition of queerness as much as it is the evergreen emotion of Catholicism. Confession and coming out go hand in hand. I feel guilty about how I express myself, the mistakes I have made, and my relationships to others. Guilt might just be my oldest companion. In a strange way, it's comforting — at the very least, I always know guilt will be there for me. Mothers hold an important place in Irish households. Mums, mams, and mas are the undeniable epicentre of everything. And as a young queer boy, my own mum came to be my best friend (indeed, it says something that she even pipped guilt to the post). When I recall childhood, my mum is a firebrand mess of gingery curls sitting on the shaggy coat printed with polar bears that I would spend hours folding myself in. Like that coat, the memory of my mum is warmth and curiosity and perfume.

As a queer person and a Catholic, one question has plagued my life: how can you be religious and LGBTQ+? This question has been posed to me just as much by my gay and lesbian brothers and sisters at dinner parties as by those involved in religious life. Yet sitting there, fork in one hand and red wine in the other, I never have a suitable answer. The dinner party is left hanging. The roast potatoes go cold. I begin to feel guilty. And who is to blame? My mum. As a child, I watched my mum approach religion with the same steely optimism with which she tackles the rest of the world. Aside from the romance of incense and the reality of hard wooden pews, my overriding recollection of church is my mum telling us she spent the service praying for our health and happiness. During contemplation, I watched as she folded into herself, kneeling on an unforgiving board in order to feather our futures with joy. Thanks to my mum, religion was always practiced with care and love and tolerance. It never occurred to me that my queerness and my faith would be at odds. Bound by so many ties, they became irreducible.

Unorthodox answers the question I have never been able to. Bringing together Christians, Hindus, Jews, Muslims and Sikhs, the pages that follow show how LGBTQ+ people of faith are negotiating their identities in Britain today. From queer priests and rabbis leading congregations in worship, to activists establishing vital networks that connect people throughout the country, to artists carving out new kinds of space in which gender, sexuality and faith can coexist. Dealing with identity, so too does this book bring together queerness and faith with race, class, disability, age, migration, health and countless other markers. Those whose stories are collected within are as contoured by family, ritual and community as they are by spirituality. What appears in this book are first-hand accounts of LGBTQ+ people boldly laying claim to faith.

This book might anger some. Not least, queer people who have faced persecution at the hands of religion. To all those who have suffered: we understand. The stories collected here are not an attempt at conversion, nor do they ignore the difficulties religion has caused. This book does not shout about joy with fingers in its ears, nor does it mine our darkest moments to find suffering. Rather, the stories contained within stem from a place of deep empathy and experience. Each of us comes to faith with eyes wide open, renegotiating what religion and spirituality mean in order to create a place that will allow us to thrive and survive. After all, hasn't this always been what the community has done? LGBTQ+ people have a history of staring rejection in the face, of turning slurs on their head and reclaiming the things from which we have been barred. Faith should be no different. It is not the job of this book to deny the difficulties religion has caused, but to turn the spotlight towards the often overlooked work of queer communities. For each evangelical denouncing abortion, there is a rabbi who quietly organised retreats for those living with HIV in the thick of the AIDS crisis. For each fundamentalist seeking to prevent sex education in schools, there is a priest fighting for changes behind the scenes.

In our contemporary moment, the connection between faith, gender and sexuality is more apparent than ever. Queer people are coming out of the closet once again by telling their friends about their connection to faith. At the same time, people of faith are queering their communities by entering into important conversations about marriage, representation and rights. And these conversations are not limited to a handful of groups. They affect all of us. Daily, we see LGBTQ+ rights being turned into political gunpowder to spread Islamophobia and antisemitism. Britain uses homophobia and transphobia to legitimise international action by denouncing the political record of other countries, all while ignoring the prejudice queer people face here today. When we present LGBTQ+ identity and faith as oppositional to each other, we erase people from the map. We lose voices that will help us build bridges. We ask people to leave behind their families, communities and support networks. Surely, queer people should be asking for increased, not diminished, power. Surely, queer people should asking to take up more, not less, space.

This call to take up more space became ever more pressing for me at London Pride. Clustered on the steps of St Martin-in-the-Fields were queer people of all stripes celebrating as the parade passed in Trafalgar Square. Puncturing the crowd, a man decked out in a sandwich board and sunhat told the revellers to repent. What did he see? Evidently, not the same scenes as most of us there. Instead of care and affection, he found sin and the opportunity to call people towards his version of faith. And yet at the bottom of the stairs, a priest was passing out rainbow face paint, wishing us well and smiling as she did so. Perhaps there is no clearer image than this hard-faced man and this smiling priest that presents the contemporary polarities queer people face when entering religious spaces. While the call to repent is all too recognisable, it is the priest's version of faith — steeped in joy and love and celebration — that resonates with my own, as well as with so many of the stories in this book. The fact that a member of the clergy would go to these lengths shows that structural changes can and are happening, that queer people are reclaiming faith.

My own faith journey is inextricably bound up with the writing of this book. For a long time, I was estranged from a faith community and from communal worship. I prayed daily and have a lasting connection with God, but the thought of church created a silence that I could not face up to. I now recognise this as a deep fear of rejection. Having spent so much time in the company of queer people of faith, however, I began exploring my own relationship with religion again, looking for spaces where I could reconnect with a community. These discussions triggered an internal searching that has led me towards the Quakers. And things are changing for me. Joining a faith community grounded in Christianity, stillness and social justice has been radically healing. Finding a community again has brought me a deep sense of joy. I owe that joy to this book and to those who sat down with me to have conversations, so thank you.

Other texts have anticipated *Unorthodox*. There have been individual recollections that capture deeply personal journeys towards faith: Lionel Blue's *A Backdoor to Heaven* (1985), Rachel Mann's *Dazzling Darkness* (2012), Amrou Al-Kadhi's *Unicorn* (2019). There have been compelling arguments for more inclusive faith: Judith Plaskow's *Standing Again at Sinai* (1990), Amir Fink and Jacob Press' *Independence Park* (2000), Pepe Hendricks' *Hijāb: Unveiling Queer Muslim Lives* (2009). There have been dialogues that connect those from across the spectrum: John McNeil's *Freedom, Glorious Freedom* (1995) and Peter Sweasey's *From Here To Eternity* (1997). Drawing on this tradition, *Unorthodox* brings together queer Christians, Hindus, Jews, Muslims and Sikhs by offering an interfaith collection of stories that reflect on the relationship between gender, sexuality and religion. Drawn from face-to-face interviews that occurred across the UK in homes, faith spaces, libraries, cafés, pubs and beyond, this book is a reclamation that shows what it means to be queer and of faith in Britain today. Together, we hope our stories hold space and create room. After all, story is the thing that grows. By telling our stories, we hope you will tell yours. We hope to make a lasting mark. We hope to continue queering religion. And I, for one, have faith that we will.

Leap of Faith

Rev. Canon Rachel Mann

I came to faith somewhat unusually. Having grown up in a family that was in some ways divided (my father was non-religious and my mother a committed Christian), I rejected faith at a relatively early age thinking that it was complete bunkum. That carried on until my twenties, when I came to a living faith in Jesus Christ. I had felt drawn to prayer for a number of years but thought, 'This is silly, I just don't think that I can believe in all this.' Ultimately, however, it became irresistible. Although I didn't know this at the time, I came to faith on the day of Pentecost, the day on which the Church celebrates the birth of the whole Church, the day on which Saint Peter stood up and said the Holy Spirit has come down upon us and called people to faith in Jesus Christ. On that day in 1996, I found I could no longer resist this call to prayer. I got down on my knees and said to God, 'If you are, then I am yours,' and had a very powerful conversion experience that utterly disrupted my life. And I am here now, in a dog collar twenty-two years later, that unusual thing: the adult convert. Most people who are adherents of any faith would say that they are cradle people, that they were formed very clearly from birth. I had a broadly Church of England upbringing, I went to a Church of England Primary School, I even took an O-level in Religious Education. Yet the fascination I felt was not the same as faith. I had rejected my faith, partly because of my gender identity, and it was not until I was a grown adult that I came to truly find faith.

I am not sure I can quite put my conversion into words. At the time I was working as a teaching fellow in philosophy at Lancaster University as part of an avowedly secular department in which there was no space for faith. My colleagues and friends would all say that they were atheists or agnostic, at best, and yet things had been changing for me for quite some time. Not least because when I was twenty-three I had transitioned from male to female, an incredibly disruptive experience. Liberating and necessary, but disruptive. Since the age of four or five I had been alert to the fact that I was going to have to address my gender dysphoria, which I lived with until I was twenty-two when I acknowledged it publicly. And that is when the wheels began to move. At twenty-three, studying for a PhD in

11

philosophy, I transitioned and in many ways my life came together. I began to be me and began to discover who I was. Pretty much anyone who has transitioned will tell you that it is not an easy thing to do and in the early 1990s it was, at times, pretty horrifying. So I was someone who had become me, but becoming me opened up all sorts of other questions about who I was in the world and about how I related to a deeper reality. That's the thing about philosophers: we ask questions. We want to interrogate the universe. We want to interrogate reality. One of my questions was 'Is there a God?' I wondered about the status of Jesus Christ and those questions simply became more and more prescient. It was like a pressure in my head. Wherever I turned, whatever I did, I seemed to return to a question mark about my desire to commit and to believe. I explored all sorts of possibilities before I did commit. I refused to believe in a Trinitarian God, that God could be simultaneously three and one, because as a philosopher you want things neat and that's a paradox. I toyed with Unitarianism, a branch of Christianity that says that Jesus isn't God but an inspired man. I toyed with Islam, because it has a clarity and simplicity to it. I was interested in Judaism. I wrote philosophical papers on the problem of the paradox of the Trinitarian God. Behind that, however, was faith.

Faith, like so many things in our life, is not rational and cannot be discovered through reason. Reason only gets us so far. Ultimately faith requires a kind of commitment, a trust, a willingness to enter into a relationship. Ironically and interestingly, as a result of becoming Rachel, of becoming me, I felt that I was substantial enough that I could let some things go. One of my favourite sentences in the Bible is when Jesus says, 'Whosoever shall seek to save his life shall lose it; and whosoever shall lose his life shall preserve it.' It's a beautiful, mysterious line, but what it fails to appreciate is that in order to let go of one's life, one has to have a life to begin with. Until I became Rachel I didn't have a life. I was just a series of masks, a series of performances in need of grounding. As Rachel I had become a person who had something to lose and it was terrifying. I thought, if I commit to God and start praying, what if God says I have made a huge mistake? What if God says that, in transitioning, I have done something terrible? What if God says 'Rachel, I love you, but you need to stop being Rachel'? There was a precipice for me. It was terrifying, but some things are irresistible. Having gone through all of this intellectual angst, emotional worry, and anxiety, that point was reached on Pentecost Sunday 1996, where having tried to resist what felt like the abyss for years, I simply could not hold on. I had to jump. Or rather, I had to leap.

There is a difference between jumping and leaping. To jump is to accept your fate, it's no more than a fall, but to leap is an intentional matter, to say, 'There is delight in this.' I leapt that night. And that experience was one I can only describe as abundant love. I thought, 'I could be giving up everything,' but what I received back was unconditional love, and I realised that I could not be the same and that I was not the same. In one sense, the old Rachel was dead, but what I had received back was so much more. Reflecting on it now, that experience was a gift. I think God offers to people the things that they need to get them going. I had been so wrapped up in the belief that God would judge me for being trans, for being queer, that I needed that experience of being utterly overwhelmed. It was an encounter with what the Romantics would call the sublime. I cannot find the words for it. The nearest I can get to it — and I appreciate that I use a term loaded with stigma — is that I went mad. That's what an encounter with the sublime is, because it takes you outside of the usual structures. I couldn't sleep that night, I was so full of delight and wonder.

The next day, I headed downstairs and I said to my mother that I had something to tell her, that I had become a Christian. She was stunned and shocked, my friends were stunned and shocked and, for those first couple of months, I thought I had lost it. I wondered if I had created a fantasy of comfort for myself, a blanket to make myself feel better about reality. I had all of those questions. When I returned to Lancaster, my friends thought I was an absolute prat. In some ways the nearest analogy is falling in love. It was like falling head over heels in love or at least that moment where you think falling head over heels is what love looks like. Of course it's not. It's a fantasy and it's unsustainable. One cannot live at that level of intensity. It has to die, has to enter into a new phase if it is going to be real love, but that's where I was. I wanted to go around and tell the world about the new love I had, Jesus Christ. I had huge falling outs: a friend and I (reconciled now) had a stand-up row about the love of Jesus Christ. I was that person who you see saying, 'Give your life to Jesus now,' but that's how love makes us behave.

One of the things that religious trans people have given a fair amount of attention to is the way in which our experiences are very much connected to religious conversion stories and rituals. There is much discussion around whether there should be renaming ceremonies or living name ceremonies for trans people in the Church, and the decision of the Church of England has been to use the reaffirmation of baptism rite. Baptism as a concept is absolutely about the death of the old self and becoming alive in Christ and the transition experience is a mirror of that. In one sense, there is this mapping together and deep integration of my experience of discovering the grace and the gift of becoming who one truly is and then discovering that who one truly is, is actually part of God's gift. It isn't about a lifestyle decision, though I think sometimes it is parodied by those who don't like trans people as pure choice. My experience of becoming me is about discovering who God has called me to be and part of the reason I am a priest is because the process of becoming a priest is another layer or another horizon of becoming more fully myself. When I talk about the old Rachel, that language reveals the extent to which my experience of being a Christian is about a journey: a journey further into the truth. The Christian formula is that everyone is made in the image of God and grows into the likeness of Christ. The Christian journey is always predicated on transformation, on conversion and (to use a very old-fashioned word that we do not like anymore) on being conformed to Christ. Now when we think of being conformed, it's about being conformist or being put in a straightjacket. We think of George Orwell's *Nineteen Eighty-Four* and everyone walking around in the same clothes. Being conformed to Christ, however, is about the way in which we become more fully our unique selves at a deep level. When Jesus says, 'Be perfect as my father is perfect,' it doesn't mean being a goodie-goodie, it means being more completely who we are called to be. When I converted and came to faith, I realised that I was still Rachel, I was absolutely Rachel, but I was more.

What I find fascinating is how my journey of conversion is also a journey of reconciliation. Indeed, I think that is the deepest call that is made upon Christians and all people of faith. Partly it is about being reconciled to God, being reconciled to the fact that we are a gift from God, and that our lives are a gift, but for me it was about being reconciled with my past, with my history and with my facticity. As a person of faith, not only did I need to be reconciled with who I had been as Rachel, I needed to be reconciled with the life that I had lived prior to transition. I had lived as a guy. I know that the current language, rightly, says that I was always Rachel, that I was always a woman, and I understand why that is the case, but I am not sure it quite captures some of the facts. Being raised as a 'boy' was deeply traumatising for me, but it's still part of the facts. The experience of coming to faith was an invitation to become ever more reconciled with my past. I wanted to push my past away. I think that's a deeply problematic thing and I think it's one of those things that our patriarchal society is obsessed with. In the days of enforced heterosexuality we were taught to push ourselves away. Now we find more creative ways of going on but, for me personally, to deal with what was dead and what was old — whether it was my dead name (the name I was given at birth) or the old Rachel — was part of my baptismal identity in Christ. It's not that somehow I became a better person, that I am more holy, more righteous or more moral. It's that I am prepared to deal with the wounds more faithfully, lovingly, tenderly, even bravely sometimes, because most of the time we do not want to go near wounds, we want to act as if we are complete and whole.

In one sense, having an encounter with the living God who said to me 'You are my beloved' has allowed me to have much more trust in who I am, to be much more accepting, to have faith in myself. There is nothing quite as powerful in some respects. Of course, it was complicated, not least because of how that is mediated on a day to day level. I was formed in a time when the narratives around transgender were very limited and I do not live in a bubble, an artificial environment or an idealised church. There is the very grit of living to contend with. The warp and weft of life to face. Living, so often for people like me, is being told that we are not very valuable, that we are rubbish, and that we exist under sufferance. I can be terrifyingly confident because I know God loves me, but the Church can be a difficult place to be different. There are lots of people in the Church who believe that God doesn't love me. Yet my position in it is hugely significant to me. For me to be a priest in the Church of God, of which the Church of England is part, isn't about a role or a job. It's about my very being. It's about who I think God has called me to be. When we talk about matters of vocation, we talk about hearing God's voice call out; to have responded to that and then have the Church recognise that call and ordain me — it's beyond words. This plays out on a very practical level. From time to time, like most clergy, I think I have had enough, I think of how the nature of the job has changed and how I could seek to do something else. I wonder about becoming a full-time writer or taking up a full-time role at a university teaching creative writing. I can go so far with that, but then what comes back is that I am a priest and whatever I was doing, at a bone deep level, I would want to offer that: to offer the gift of prayer, to preside at mass, to conduct weddings and funerals, and to be there at people's most painful and most joyous moments. That won't go away. So right in the midst of some of the worst times — and sometimes it is very hard, ministry is not an easy thing to do — I say, 'But I am a priest.' Even if I were teaching creative writing, I would still be a priest. I would grieve if there were no way I could exercise my ministry. Just as I feel that I have to write, I feel compelled to have this identity. Being a priest is different to being a rector of a parish or a canon of a cathedral. A priest refers to one's basic identity as a minister, whereas rector or canon refers to the role occupied. It's comparable with being in the army. All those who hold commissions are officers, but a captain or colonel occupy different roles or ranks. Those are jobs that one exercises. Yet none of that could happen without this deep sense that I have been recognised as having a valid call by the Church of God, that I have been ordained and that in that ordination there is a sense that I have become more fully who God wants me to be. Just as much as transitioning has become life-saving, enriching and transforming, so has becoming a priest.

As I came to faith I began to have a sense of being called to priesthood. Initially I thought this was disturbing. I believed I was just a vain egotist who needed to be at the front and that I wouldn't be happy 'sitting in the pews'. However, I was encouraged to explore that vocation and that led to some surprising turns. I left the world of the university in 1997 and moved to inner-city Salford. I was supposed to be there for a year with other Christians exploring their vocation to priesthood. I ended up staying six years. In that time I continued exploring my calling to vocation, though I faced many knockbacks. In 1999 the diocese believed that I was a good candidate but that they did not believe at that time the church could affirm a trans person as a priest. Simultaneously I became desperately ill with Crohn's disease, which meant that I could not work for years. I resumed the vocational journey in 2001, taking on a demanding job as a civil servant working with the homeless to prove that I could handle difficult work.

In 2003 I reached my selection conference, a three-day event at which representatives of the Church decide whether to recommend people for training as priests. I believed the Church was going to say no. Although I was very experienced by that point, having had a lot of lay roles, I was still trans of course. Just before the conference began however, I was given a secret piece of paper that indicated that the bishops of the Church of England had privately talked about the status of trans people. To my shock it was a very positive and affirming document. I later discovered that it had been partly written by one of my former psychiatrists when I had been going through the transition program who had been incredibly supportive and was a Christian himself. I like to feel that he remembered me when they were putting that paper together. So I went to the selection conference and was recommended to training — much to my profound surprise and terror. I thought, 'I might actually have to do this now.' I was sent to Birmingham where I trained for two years. In 2005 I was ordained Deacon and 2006 ordained Priest. From 2005 I was curate (a training priest position) in Stretford, South Manchester and then in 2008 I was appointed incumbent rector at St Nicholas Burnage, where I have been for nearly ten years. In that time I have held down many different roles, including poet in residence at Manchester Cathedral. It has been quite a long process of coming to where I am now.

There are of course many layers to being a priest. Practically, it involves being the leader of not just a church but a parish. I am licensed to a geographical location: I have the spiritual care of anyone who lives in Burnage. It doesn't matter if they believe in God; it doesn't matter if they are Christian, Muslim, Sikh or Hindu; it's part of the nature of the Church of England as the established Church. I am licensed to care for the whole of this parish and that's what I do. Basically every day my first job is to pray. That is my first calling. Each day I pray for the parish, for the world, for people in need. My second role is to prepare people for death. What that means for me is to be a pastor, primarily to my congregation at St Nicholas, but it also means going out and visiting the sick and needy, and making hospital visits. It sounds a bit of a grim task but really it's about helping people to understand who they are and the way of the world. And that breaks down in lots of other ways. It involves preaching. It involves being the chief minister at the mass or the Eucharist. It involves being the chief minister in baptism. It involves conducting funerals. It involves taking weddings. When I was a curate, my boss said to me, 'Love people, Rachel, and let them love you. That's the job of being a priest.' So it's my job to love people even when they are not terribly lovable. That's what I try to do. Now, of course, if you are a priest of a landmark building as I am (St Nicholas is a nationally significant architectural gem), you are also a manager. Part of my job inevitably is to raise lots and lots of money to protect the building. It's a demanding role. As a parish priest, and this is very much a Church of England thing, I also try and be available to the wider community. I am the chair of trustees of our local foodbank. The foodbank is an independent charity, not a religious thing, but I am the chair. It's my commitment. I work with local councillors to ensure that this area is a good place to live. It's that kind of involvement in the community that's important.

As there are many roles to being a priest, there are many lines to being a queer person of faith. To be a priest who is queer is always to be othered. I do not inhabit the normative position of who a priest is. In the Church of England, still, priests are usually white, middle-class, male, married with kids. I am white and middle-class, but to be queer and to be out and proud is to be othered. I think being othered has all sorts of peculiar effects. When I was recommended for training by the diocese, I was guaranteed a job. Some people would say that's fantastic, that I was assured of a job at the end of the training process. I have to say, it did make me feel relaxed in some respects, but actually it's a signal of othering as well. It's a signal that I could not be treated equally with other people. Even if that has a good effect, it's also one that makes me feel uncomfortable. And it's something that came back to me again and again during my first eight years of being ordained. I was treated differently from other priests. That is difficult. On the one hand there might be positive elements but many are negative. One such element was the Church asking, 'Rachel, how do we deal with what people say about you?' I was encouraged not to talk about being trans and that creates a silencing effect. There's an anxiety around how people will react if they don't know you. Will they see my transness first rather than the loving person that I am (or some people say I am, anyway)? So there was this public silence about being trans, which is a difficult negotiation for trans people. This feeds into notions of stealth and passing, which can be controversial in the trans community. At one level, I had spent a lot of time being stealthy (not being open about my trans identity) because I could get away with it, but there were always side effects to that, such as feeling a kind of shame and wondering, 'Oh God, what if I am exposed?' So I carried within me a lot of internalised issues as I entered ministry and there were these acres of silence. I would tell individuals but there was this element of embarrassment about coming out. When should I come out? What should I say?

There was a big issue at one point surrounding a course I was teaching that was run by the diocese. It was a course in which people shared an awful lot and it was expected that people could handle the complexities of people's stories. Right at the end of that course when people were talking about sexuality and gender, I disclosed to the group that I was trans. Someone complained about me to the senior staff. Though I was not told about this complaint, the fallout was that I was quietly not asked to be involved in leading the course again. I am delighted to say that has been resolved, but I had to go into the lion's den to resolve it. I had to face down bishops. That's a horrible position to be placed in. And if it's horrible for me, then it must be terrible for people in a less privileged position than me.

In 2012 I reached a point where I had turned forty and begun to wonder who I was going to be in the world. I had been slowly disclosing much more about myself: I had gone from writing anonymously about being trans to putting my name to things, though mostly in an academic sense. I didn't want to be one of those semi-closeted people that the Church specialises in, because it still has this gift of doing the 'Don't Ask Don't Tell' thing. There are still so many clergy, certainly of an older generation, who would never acknowledge their partners or come out to their congregations or the wider world. That's fair enough, the Church is not an easy place to be, but it's also costly. I had decided I needed to be clear about who I am so I wrote a book, *Dazzling Darkness*, essentially my spiritual autobiography up until that point, a theological memoir. The side effects of that were interesting because I really nailed my colours to the mast and it led to all sorts of repercussions, good and ill, in the local church, the national Church and the international Church. It is a book I am really proud of and a book that was necessary for me to write, but it revealed something about my congregation that I hadn't realised. Some people would say that they were affirming of LGBT people but they didn't want to have to face the implications of what that would mean if they had someone who was actually like that in their congregation. There were sticky moments. It was uncomfortable. It wasn't that I would lose my job (I had the support of my bishop in publishing the book) but it meant that we had to do some work on accepting difference, which we continue to do. Now we have become a congregation where people are very much out about who they are. In a sense, coming out as trans has given people permission to be out not just about their gender or sexuality but about all sorts of things. It's felt like a much healthier congregation and has had an effect on the wider community.

Nonetheless, writing a book like *Dazzling Darkness* also makes one a target in the internet age. Of course — I say of course, I shouldn't have to say of course — I have been a target for nastiness. I have been ridiculed by ultra-conservative Christians. I have been told that I should be defrocked and barred from being a priest. Last year I was number eight on a list of a hundred reasons that the Church of England is falling apart. I was sad that I was only number eight! I have received death threats, which has entailed getting the police involved. I have been deliberately misgendered. All that is costly. In some respects I can live with it better than some people because I grew up in a world without the internet and social media, so though it is massively influential on my life now my core identity was formed in a world before all that happened. What is really interesting is when things get reported to you. A member of our local congregation was telling me a story of how she went to another church for an event and got talking to a member of that congregation. The conversation turned to where she went to church and who her minister was. When she told them that her priest was Rachel Mann, it turned into a rant about how disgusting I was and how this other person would never come to anything that would be held at St Nicholas. Luckily, I don't have to live with that nastiness on a day-to-day level because, frankly, what people respond to is your love and your care. When you are face to face with someone it is really difficult for them to be horrid, but it's still costly.

I was involved with the Church of England's Shared Conversation process, which developed to try and find a way forward through the current impasse around the status of LGBT people in the Church, triggered largely by changes in the law around marriage in 2013. The nature of the Shared Conversation was to get people from a whole range of perspectives within the Church together to speak openly and honestly about who they are and hopefully build relationships. My experience of the process was okay, but I will never forget a moment when we were broken into trios and given half an hour to speak without interruption and say exactly what we thought. One person was just vile, a bigot as far as I was concerned. To have to sit there and hear that and not be able to challenge it was a reminder than there are people who, in my view, are so broken and wounded and damaged that they cannot even acknowledge people like me as full human beings. That's costly to live with and be in the same room as.

I have kept going because of the abundance of God's love. I am determined to say that even with those who do not want to acknowledge my full humanity and my full status of a child of God, I want to acknowledge theirs. That is so costly. It is sorely tested (and frankly, sometimes the only way for me to deal with it is to not get too close to them) but I want to say that it is the nature of the Church, as a gift from God, that it is not a place simply filled with lovely people or those that are the same as me. It is a place where God wishes to hold all of us in our complexity, in our damage. I am as kooky, as damaged, and broken as the rest but I just happen to think that my brokenness doesn't lie in my gender identity because that is a gift. Of course, I am as screwed up as the next person, but if God can be faithful to someone as screwed up as me then God can be faithful to someone that is screwed up so much that they think that someone being gay is wicked and monstrous. I want to stick with it because God sticks with it and I want to be faithful to God, but of course it is hard. Sometimes the analogy I want to use is family, a complicated notion because the family can be the springboard for our greatest triumphs but also the location of our greatest trauma. As much as I adore my parents, my brother and my sister, would I want to spend every day with them for the rest of my life? Of course I wouldn't, nor would they with me. That applies even more so with the extended family. There are some really fruity people in my extended family (and from their point of view I am really fruity too) but we are still family. There is scope and space for us to all hold together. So from the fieriest bishop right through to the loveliest old lady right through to me, we are still part of God's family. If God sticks with that family, I'll do my utmost to stay. And if I don't stay, if people like us don't stay, then we are just giving into the bastards.

I really respect people who say they have to leave. I really respect LGBT people who say, 'Enough of this.' If someone is being abused or has had that experience, then do everything you can to get away from that abuse and survive. If you need to dish out some comeback against the person or the institution that has abused you, then you have my support. In my experience however there is still sufficient grace in the church community. I have met some of the most gracious, beautiful, wondrous and saintly people in church communities; they remain one of those rare places where you get intergenerational relationships, where you can get class relationships that aren't based on networks — and in our increasingly networked world, there is something really powerful about communities which seek to model a kind of difference at their heart. I suppose if you want a theological reason for staying it is that difference. Where better for a queer person to be than in the queerest community of all? There is nowt queerer than the Christian God, who is both three yet one. This community of love: father, son, and Holy Spirit, dancing in and through each other and yet is absolutely one. That's the queerest thing imaginable. We have a queer God who calls us into queer community. That's the church at its best.

At the heart of Christianity is Jesus Christ. He represents the very heart of God, not through turning up in a chariot as a great general or even as a king fighting off all others, but as a Palestinian peasant in a precarious situation. According to the Biblical accounts he was born in an outhouse and laid in a manger, profoundly vulnerable, a baby utterly dependent on others. It is the nature of being a baby that you are not going to survive without the love and care of someone to look after you. And he grows into someone who, again, does not become a great general, king, leader or even prophet in the traditional sense but someone who, at his best, gathers twelve apostles and one hundred and forty-four other disciples around him. His voice does not carry far. He is not a privileged person. He ultimately dies a criminal's death. Insofar as he heals the wounds of the world, takes away the sin of the world, it's done through his broken body. When he comes to us in resurrection, again, it is not as some sort of Greek god, immortal, hard, untouchable and capricious, but as one who bears the wounds of our violence against him in our risen flesh. If Jesus is the model for all Christians and therefore all priests, I think we are called to model someone who does not present a macho mentality but one which exposes our wounds. Someone who says that through our wounds we are more exposed to each other. It's about relationship. Christianity is all about relationship: with other people, but more importantly with God. It's outrageous that God comes to us in the form of a human being. It makes a radical claim.

There is a mission that God is calling me to undertake. It brings me great hope that I do that without having to pretend to be something other than I am. And it gives others permission. When I stand up to preach and preside at the altar, it's as me. I am saying to others: You are called to be you, be you as you worship God, God delights in you as you are. I think being a priest is about being vulnerable. Vulnerability means being open. The Latin *vulnus* means wound. That's the thing about wounds, they can repel us and terrify us because they are a sign of our weakness, our mortality and our limit. Yet they are also places that open us up to other possibilities. I have had such major wounds in my life as a result of surgery that they have had to be laid open, sometimes for months, so that they can heal properly. They need to be exposed to the air, exposed to other possibilities. It's important. Sometimes people say Christianity has a downer on the body but I don't think it does. It's about the facts of the body. It says that salvation is wrought through a body, the body of Jesus Christ. That must say that the body is a moment of glory but also that salvation is wrought through limit, through living in this world. As a priest I would go so far as to say that I am called to be an icon of Christ and a sign of the church, what I am called to represent is this particular body that I am, with all its glory and all its grace, but also with all its limits and vulnerability. God calls particular people to be priests. There is no such thing as being a priest in general, it is all about acting as the priest God has called you to be. If I acted as if I wasn't this body then I would be betraying that call. This body is a disabled body, a damaged body, a chronically ill body, a trans body. If a priest is a sign of Christ then doesn't that suggest that Christ is disabled, is trans, is chronically ill? He can hold all of that within the depth of his being.

Maryam Din (photo: Jazz Glenn)

Our Own Histories

Maryam Din

This Ramadan has felt important to me in a way that it hasn't before. I feel that previously I've just been going through the motions — I didn't eat during daylight hours because my family were fasting. However, Ramadan is so much bigger than that. Fasting is one of the five pillars of Islam and is a vehicle for being able to participate in the other aspects of Ramadan. Often people have this idea that you fast to walk a mile in someone else's shoes, to understand what it's like for the poor who don't have food and to show solidarity. That's not only wrong, it's offensive. What does that mean for poor people who are observing Ramadan? Does that mean they can't observe? Of course it doesn't! That's not the point of fasting.

Fasting during Ramadan isn't to show solidarity with the needy or so that we can understand what it's like to be in their shoes and to understand the importance of giving to charity. Zakat, the purification of wealth, is another pillar of Islam. Muslims are required to give up 2.5% of their annual income to charity if they can afford to. More money tends to be given to charity during Ramadan. Ramadan isn't religious #activism. I understand the sentiment and I know it comes from a good place, but that's not what it's about. The Qur'an clearly states in Surah Baqarah, 'You who believe, fasting is prescribed for you, as it was prescribed for those before you, so that you may be mindful of God.' As in other faiths, we fast to learn self-restraint and discipline and to create a consciousness of God. Ramadan is a blessed month where we all have an opportunity to better ourselves. It's about self-reflection, it's about patience, it's about taking the time out to think and to pray in order to become better Muslims and members of our communities. The hope is to sustain this throughout the year. It's important to understand and to recognise that those who are exempt from fasting for health reasons are still able to reap the rewards and blessings this Holy Month has to offer.

This Ramadan felt different for a few reasons. I feel my intentions were different this year. I might not have prayed more, but I've definitely been more self-reflective and wanting to change certain patterns of behaviour. I had an important conversation with a friend and her faith inspired me. She spoke passionately about Islam, so much so that I was surprised she had not converted yet (she had even chosen a Muslim name). I could feel her passion and it lit a fire in me too. I was supporting and encouraging her which felt a little strange as I feel like I'm not there yet with my own faith. I find myself being so envious of people who have a strong connection with their faith and with Allah (Subhanahu wa ta'ala). As well as this, my mum has recently come back from pilgrimage in Saudi Arabia, she completed Umrah and I really wanted to go with her.

What's interesting is that usually when you go on pilgrimage, you are already at a point with your religion where your faith is pretty strong. Why else would you pay a few thousand pounds to go? It's not a decision to be taken lightly. However, for me, it felt different: this is a journey that I'm on right now. I'm really intrigued and inspired by Islam, I want to learn more and to be more participatory. I feel like doing pilgrimage would be an excellent way to do that. Aside from it being a pillar of faith, pilgrimage is important to me because there are so many millions of people around the world who come to this one place. There are so many different cultures and languages, and you might not understand the person who's standing next to you, but you have your religion in common and you're all praying to Allah. This is powerful in terms of our interconnectedness and the human condition. It seems cheesy, but I really value and thrive from deep human connection. I treasure meeting people and forging new relations, whether it's friendship, or a more intimate relationship, or meeting a stranger on the train — it's finding something meaningful to bond over. That sense of union and shared experiences is even stronger when people come together with a common purpose, and I can't comprehend what that feeling must be like when it has a religious dynamic. It makes me think about the potential and power when striving for social justice. My mum is thinking about going on Hajj soon and I hope to join her.

As a kid, I knew I was different and eventually realised that I am queer. As an adult, I've been very vocal, speaking out against all forms of intolerance, bigotry, Islamophobia, racism and fascism, while also being heavily involved in the LGBTQ community. The first struggle came when I was discovering my sexuality. I didn't have anyone that looked like me around, so I genuinely thought you couldn't be queer and a Muslim, or of any faith. I didn't see how it worked. I didn't see any examples around me of how these identities co-existed. The main narrative is that they are antithetical. The realisation that you can be LGBTQ and practice religion was really important.

When I was studying for my undergraduate degree, I was at a local gay bar with a friend and got chatting to a woman I'd met a couple of times before. It was some ridiculous time in the morning, 1am or 2am. I don't drink, she was a little tipsy, and the conversation we were having at this very early hour was about faith. She was sharing with me that she was a lesbian and that when she came out to her congregation, they ostracised her. I always feel a profound sadness when people share these stories with me. It would be one thing if she had stopped believing in God, but she stopped going to church because of how the congregation treated her. I don't agree with the premise that it's a sin, but even if religious people consider being LGBTQ to be sinful, you don't shun people even if you think they are sinning. Why is it that being an LGBTQ person of faith is suddenly the worst thing? Something that you don't want in your congregation? Surely, you want to bring people in?

What draws me to Islam is social justice. There's a great book by Scott Siraj Al-Haqq Kugle called *Homosexuality in Islam: Critical Reflection on Gay, Lesbian, and Transgender Muslims*. It's a thick text that talks about many things but, in particular, the idea of liberation theology. The book argues that liberation theology tries to 'restore the courage of those who are oppressed, confident that those who suffer truly understand God's message and, in standing against such injustice, embody God's will in this world.' That is a powerful statement, because when we look at the Abrahamic religions, which I know most about, the prophets and the holy people walked with the most marginalised in their communities. When we look at religions today, I don't feel they are following the same ethos. That's a problem for me. If you're not walking with the most marginalised people, whose side are you on? Jesus was out there chilling with sex workers. These are the same people that are shunned in today's society. It's not what religion or faith is about.

Last year, I went to Rome and to the Vatican City. It's amazing, the grandeur, the art, it's decorated in gold! But there were homeless people right outside the walls of the city. There is something categorically wrong for that dichotomy to exist. The fact that the prophets and the holy people were poor says a lot. This might upset some people, but, at their core, the Abrahamic religions are socialist religions. There is a massive disconnect with the founding principles and beliefs within religions and how people are choosing to practice them today.

It's poignant that Islam started as a protest against a system of oppression. Muslims were suffering as an oppressed minority, which is why they left Mecca and moved to Medina, founding a commonwealth. That migration set the precedent for what Islam is about. It was about breaking down divisions and barriers. The Qur'an encourages solidarity with the oppressed. We have a responsibility as people of faith to stand with the marginalised. I am reminded of the Christian poem 'Footprints in the Sand', where a person is going through hardship and he asks God, 'Where were you in my time of need? Why was there only one set of footprints in the sand?' and God answers, 'I was carrying you, that is why there was only one set of footprints.' That's so powerful because there is a different level of understanding that people have when they are going through hardship. A connection not only with other people, but also with the divine. As Scott Siraj Al-Haqq Kugle says, 'The story of the Prophets is the narrative of those who hear the speech of God because their ears are opened by suffering, oppression and struggling against it with endurance and patience.' It's about sacrificing your wellbeing to protect others. It's wholesome to think that those who are on the fringes of society should be intrinsically valued within religion.

I'm vocal about being queer and Muslim because there aren't enough people who look like me. Having a platform to talk about these topics means that I'm in a privileged position. Visibility is important. Visibility saves lives. If there were more people that looked like me when I was growing up, my own journey might have been more comfortable. Difference and diversity is great for communities and societies. We need more of it as it enriches all our lives. I think there is difficulty in mainstream religion for queer people to find a space because of how cis (cisgender: identifying with the gender you were assigned at birth) and heteronormative religious spaces are. That's not a commentary on the religion itself, but on the congregation. That's why groups like the Inclusive Mosque Initiative matter greatly, helping to create and carve out spaces where people feel comfortable and at ease to be able to foster a relationship with Allah. That's another thing about Islam that I love, there's no hierarchy of faith. There are people that are more learned, scholars and the like, but when you pray it is literally just you and God, there is no intermediary, it's a direct relationship. Ideally, the endpoint would be for people to feel comfortable in more mainstream spaces, but that depends on where you find yourself on the gender and sexuality spectrum. It's a safety issue. The more visibly queer we are in comparison to our assigned gender, the more difficulties we face in terms of how the world interacts with us and how comfortable we feel in certain spaces.

We all deserve to have a relationship with Allah and nobody has ownership of religion. Islam has a rich tapestry of sexual and gender diversity. Prophet Muhammad (Peace Be Upon Him) supported and protected those at the fringes of society. He was proactive in defending sexual and gender minorities and human rights. He protected and housed trans and queer people, he welcomed them into his home. Western Christian colonisation has a lot to answer for; it infected Islam in many ways and the ramifications are still being felt today.

We need to pick up the books ourselves, we need to read, and learn our own faiths, religions and histories. Whether it's a holy book or another text, reading opens our hearts and minds. After all, knowledge is power. The very fact that the Qur'an is written in questions means that it wants you to question what it is that you are reading. Allah instructs us not follow blindly the religion of our parents or our kin. How can you fulfil this request without questioning? Islam has a tradition of ijtihad, of independent reasoning. It's arguable that the tradition of open and free thinking went when Prophet Muhammad died as he was no longer there to guide people, but we can revive that ancient tradition. People can become quite defensive when matters close to their heart are critiqued. With respect to culture and religion this is particularly understandable given the ever-increasing rise of far-right extremism. However, in this discussion, religion isn't about blindly following a set of rules with no compassion, openness or tolerance for questions.

Last year, I visited the Museum of Science and Technology in Islam while in Istanbul, and it was fascinating. Initially, I was really annoyed because the first room was filled with bronze 3D portraits of white non-Muslim Europeans and I couldn't understand why the curators would have made this decision. I expected better from a Muslim majority country. In the next room was a video explaining the reason and scope of the exhibition and the significance of these European faces. The video explained that Muslim scientists would cite their predecessors and those whose work they were building on and further explained that the Westerners were bigoted and kept shady the great achievements of Muslim scholars. Europeans would cite the Ancient Greeks as the creators and masterminds of inventions that the Arabs and Muslims had created, and they re-wrote history. Imagine having such a superiority complex! It came to light that had it not been for these men who diligently tried to spread the work of Arabs and Muslims throughout the Western world, much of this work would have been lost forever. It's important to learn and teach history, especially in a climate where the narrative is to rewrite the past to make yourself look bigger and better.

Aside from that, the museum was incredible: science, dentistry, astrology, architecture. The things that moved me most were the inception of Arabic numbers, the wealth of knowledge and research on astrology and that the surgical implements invented wouldn't look out of place in operating theatres today. The work that was done in the Golden Age of Islam is amazing and people need to know this history, to know the contributions that other civilisations have made to the world and not just what European colonisers want you to know. Many of us know about Newton, Aristotle, Einstein, Pythagoras, Darwin, but how many people know of non-European scientists who made great scientific contributions such as al Jahith, Ibn al-Haytham, al-Zahrawi, Jabir ibn Hayyan and ibn Sina? Many scientific discoveries cited as European and Greek were actually discovered centuries earlier by Arabs and Muslims.

When it comes to community, I feel a part of all of them and none of them. Being part of the South Asian diaspora as British Asian, while also being Muslim and a part of the LGBTQ community, comes with challenges. I also feel a great sense of pride and power with respect to the energy, activism and love that flows out of marginalised communities, though sometimes I feel too brown in some spaces, too Muslim in others and too queer elsewhere. I often think about belonging and what that means for people on the fringes of society. The communities I feel most comfortable in are those that are diverse in culture, ethnicity and religion. I find community among those who are striving and fighting for social justice. Community is about creating and making space. I don't mind if people don't understand things, so long as there is a propensity for learning. We're all learning! However, in terms of the wider LGBTQ community, I do feel it's racist, with microaggressions and lack of understanding of people of colour.

Last year at a Pride event, I gave a speech that fell very flat. The person before me gave a speech about knowing your history, which was great, and I was speaking about the same thing and went into more depth. I talked about how I believe the police should not be welcome to march at Pride. I don't expect applause when I speak, but there was silence. I was looking out to this largely white crowd and remember thinking, 'I have said an uncomfortable truth.' People like me — people of colour, or of faith, or from immigrant backgrounds — don't feel safe around the police. I don't care whether they have community outreach programmes or if individual officers are great or if those officers are LGBTQ or Muslim themselves, because when they put on that uniform, they are no longer an individual and instead become an agent of the state. I know that there are police officers who are trying to make changes and do positive things, but the police aren't there to serve those on the fringes of society. The police are there to serve the policies of whatever government is in power. Currently, it's a Conservative government and we know how they treat LGBTQ people, how they treat people of colour, how they treat immigrants and how they treat refugees. Over the past few years, the government have deported many LGBTQ asylum seekers back to countries where they will most certainly face death. These are often countries where the British Empire imposed anti-homosexuality laws. So when I say no police at Pride, it's for a reason.

I think my speech fell flat on its face because of the tone of the mainstream LGBTQ community. It is a problem. On the one hand, Pride is amazing because we have come so far in our march for human rights and have so much to be proud of and celebrate. It's been an incredible, difficult and deeply profound journey, but we still have so far to go. Pride has become very whitewashed, very corporate and centred around partying. Equal marriage was hardly the last barrier for equality and liberation. I would like to get married one day, but what about trans rights? What about non-binary people? What about institutional racism? What about our NHS and the way this government treats people from lower socio-economic backgrounds? All of these issues are interconnected and I feel like people often look at them individually, when we exist in many different identities, backgrounds and communities. For example, I am a first generation, queer Muslim woman of colour from Kashmir. These issues overlap, we can't look at them as single issues. As Audre Lorde says, 'There is no such thing as a single-issue struggle because we do not live single-issue lives.' Our lives are intersectional and the issues and injustices we face can only be tackled by looking at them in this way. Social justice and human rights advocacy demand this.

There is always more that can be done, that must be done. It upsets me when minority communities show bigotry and intolerance towards other minority communities, irrespective of whether they fit into that community. When I see LGBTQ people being racist, it upsets me more than when cis straight white people do it. As LGBTQ people, we understand what it means to be marginalised. We should know better. I feel the exact same frustration when I see people of colour who weren't even born here (not that that would have justified their discrimination) lambasting the rise of Eastern European immigration, not realising or appreciating the contribution that people from all walks of life make to our country in terms of diversity, culture, knowledge and skills.

We need to acknowledge and challenge each other's privileges. All of us have privilege and power to some degree, even if it's very small and even if it's in just one space. It's about utilising our voices and challenging things. In order to fight any kind of intolerance, bigotry or oppression, we need the main group on side. Whether it's been the black civil rights movement or fighting for women's rights, we have always needed the mainstream population's support. Now, with the LGBTQ community, we need LGBTQ people to listen to those who are on the fringes of the community itself and within wider society. We need to move away from feeling uncomfortable about talking about certain topics. People are worried about offending, even if their heart is in the right place, and that stops the conversation from even starting. We need to get over that. If people come with the right intentions and an open heart, even if they don't have the right language, we can talk about that and work through it together. The onus needs to be on those who have more privilege to do the work, to be brave and to face their fears about saying the wrong thing, rather than putting the onus on the marginalised group — we need to subvert the power dynamic. We can educate people in a wholesome way. We can call people in when necessary and create that safe space to educate, challenge and thrive with a view to changing communities and wider society for the better.

All this comes back to social justice for me. I have a real passion for social justice and community work. Whether it's in co-creating QTIPOC Notts (Queer, Trans, Intersex People of Colour Nottingham) or organising vigils and protests, social justice stands out for me as a Muslim and as a member of wider communities. My queerness only strengthens that resolve. I feel like I have a unique perspective that allows me to connect with others. There is intimacy, vulnerability and interconnectedness in being a queer Muslim woman. It makes me who I am and I think others recognise and resonate with that. A couple of years ago, when I was struggling with my faith, a friend who I consider way more religious than me said, 'Out of all of the friends that I have, I would consider you to be the most religious.' My friend said that it was because of my character, and it was a deeply profound moment for me, especially as someone who, for a long time, felt that that they couldn't even be Muslim. To hear that I was what Islam looked like to someone else was incredibly powerful and moving. You can be LGBTQ and religious. There is room for everyone. Allah loves us all. If Muslims want to follow early Islamic culture and Prophet Muhammad's life, then they must support and defend those on the fringes of society, support sexual and gender minorities and champion human rights and liberation for all.

Jaivant Patel (photo: Matthew Cawrey)

Dance is My Devotion

Jaivant Patel

I want to start with a story. I was once at a hen party where I met someone who is a part of my community but who I didn't know at the time. She came up to me and said, 'Your consciousness has an extremely strong relationship with Shiva. My intuition and psychic nerves kick in around strong personalities, I don't broadcast it because people are very cynical, but you should go to the temple to worship Shiva.' Up until that point, I had never really connected with the deity Shiva. I had never ignored him, but it wouldn't come across my mind to worship him. I grew up in a Vaishnava tradition; it was Krishna whom my grandma was devoted to so that was the tradition I knew. Yet I remembered a film on VHS that my grandfather bought from the shop during a festival. It was about Shiva and his consort Parvati. I remember at one point they came into one being so that they were half-man and half-woman, Ardhanarishwara. I found the concept strange and did not understand it but there was something in me that fully connected with it because of the duality.

At the hen party, I was told that I should go the temple every Monday to practice Shiva Pujan, pouring milk on the Shivling to worship Shiva. Doing so opened my eyes. Gradually I felt that something awoke in me and I began to become more confident in who I was. Once while I was performing the ritual another woman was watching me. This was nothing new, I am used to people staring at me, but afterwards she told me that she found my worship moving and that she saw it as a beautiful dance. That brought something home because Shiva is the god of dance and I think of dance as my devotion. Dance is an expression of my faith. Dance allows me to connect to a higher plane. It is my shraddha and my puja. It is my liberation. I feel free when I am on stage, I feel like I can fly. I do not even see the audience, I am under the lights trying to connect with a higher presence and connect with who I am. Dance allows me to communicate what I cannot always express in words to the audience, regardless of whether I have blocked them out or not.

As a child, things were not always like this. I was born into my faith. Hinduism is my family religion and very much a part of Gujarati culture within the Indian subcontinent. Luckily, the majority of my upbringing was with my grandma, which influenced me heavily. My grandma showed me things and taught me lessons, told me about the gods of the Indian Pantheon, religious stories, and mythology. I loved watching my grandma get dressed, the beautiful sari with all its folds and all her jewellery. Through my grandma, I also took part in all the festivals. I knew about why we celebrated Diwali, Navaratri, Dushero, Durgasthami, Jana-masthami. I sat at home and watched Mahabharata on BBC2 and Ramayan when it was televised. At that point, however, my religion was very ritualistic. It was black and white — I did not have a deeper understanding. And I did not dance. I always wanted to be a dancer but I was never allowed to because boys do not dance, especially due to the stigma of it within the Indian culture. That stigma still exists but less so now compared to when I was growing up.

Then came the adolescent stage of my life. As a teenager, I began to struggle to accept who I was as a person in regards to my sexuality. I did not understand what being gay meant but I knew that I was different. There were no role models around whom I could associate with and connect to. It was difficult. There were gay people, of course, but there were not any Indian gay people who were out in the open and that I could look up to, let alone people from my own faith. I went through a period of rediscovery and for a long time questioned my faith, which came to a head when I came out at the age of fourteen to my mum (who did not take it very well). This pivotal point in my life happened to arrive at a moment when I discovered performing arts. At this point, I grabbed the bull by its horns. I chose drama at GCSE, allowing me to go on and study Performing Arts at A-level. Finally, I could express myself and be who I wanted to be in a safe environment, though there were still limitations.

After leaving college, I won a place at the Northern School of Contemporary Dance in Leeds. Though I had no dance training, they saw my potential and I got in. I started seeing people of many different cultures and faiths from many different background and countries. It was a shock. That is when I really started living my life as a gay man. I do not want to give the impression that I was brought up in a rigid environment, because I was not, but I had the burden of society, of judgement, and of perception. At the Northern School I could be free. Within the space of those four years, I lived my gay life: I went out clubbing and I had many flings. I was able to express myself and, because of this, I started to discover my dance body and to find out who I was as an artist. I was not a popular dancer at the Northern School — I had many friends but I was never the go-to dancer — yet this meant that I was able to sit back and observe how others worked in the studios and during performances, giving me an understanding of the mechanics of dance. That was until my third year, when Jeremy Nelson came to choreograph the final year show. We clicked. A trio I was in was given a prominent role in the graduation show and my trio was the central phrase throughout the whole of the piece. We went on tour and it was really beautiful to be a part of.

Finishing at the Northern School of Contemporary Dance in 2004, I came back to Wolverhampton. It was less constraining than I remembered it to be, but it was still restrictive. I promised that I would not shy away from who I was. I might not have admitted my sexuality to everybody, because I did not see that as anybody's business, but I would conduct myself professionally and at the same time not shy away from who I was personally. I started working within the community more, teaching the Diwali show and teaching children. That came with some battles, especially within my community. Some people were shocked that there was a gay man teaching their children. Luckily my work stood through and people saw what I was able to do. I am thankful for that decision because it has made me the out and proud gay man I am now, however at the time I had a lot going on mentally.

This led me to understand who I was as a dancer, as well as someone who identifies as being Indian, because that is a complex thing within contemporary dance. The world of dance is still very Western-centric and not always aware of or sympathetic to diverse intersectionality. If you are Indian, people assume that your training is going to be in a classical Indian dance form or in something ethnic, but mine was the opposite way. When I left the Northern School of Contemporary Dance, I went to an audition for a production that had a South Asian narrative within it. I was told that I did not need to audition because they presumed I would have South Asian training. On that proviso, I did not take the role. Integrity is very important to me as an artist, so I said no to the job. Yes, I do look at Indian dance to inform my work, aesthetics, and principles but it is a reference point, like a blood memory. It is inherent in me: the art of dance makes me want to connect with my cultural references regardless of whether I have experienced or trained within them.

There are still huge issues around the exoticism and appropriation of South Asian work. Similarly, no one wants to explore the deeper or more meaningful qualities beyond the face value of things. For example, in the past I have pitched my work to LGBT festivals but it is not queer enough for them. It is not loud or wild enough. In itself, there are many questions about what these festivals mean and whom they are for. Representation is a problem. I think it comes down to education and how much people are actually informed. At the same time, on the other side of the coin is Section 377 in India, which has ramifications in the Western and South Asian world. Within Indian culture, the LGBT community has not always felt able to come out. The diaspora that came to the UK did not have the burden of a law that forbade homosexuality because it was decriminalised in 1967 around the time the first wave of Indian immigration began. In 2009, India decriminalised Section 377 but it was recriminalised in 2013. Only in 2018 was it totally wiped out by the Supreme Court. Seeing the diaspora's reaction to that has been really interesting. When a law in India changes, it automatically feeds into the diasporic community and I have seen a shift happening. You can still feel colonialism's legacy on different communities that stem from the same culture.

In my communities, I am half-accepted. When you grow up as a gay man, you have to validate who you are through your work and your actions. Being Indian and being South Asian in the dance world, you have to work twice as hard to show why you deserve to be there. Being a minority in that sector you have to work to get your craft out, to get people to understand who you are beyond the exoticism and appropriation. I believe a lot of this is about pre-colonial rule. In India, you visit temples, you see the Kama Sutra on the temple walls, you gain a sense of the idea that gender did not exist. I believe the idea of conforming to gender-specific roles was brought on by the British colonisation of India. It is as simple as that. During pre-colonial rule, India identified a third gender, which I believe in the modern world has become somewhat misconstrued. The third gender was all about the other, individuals who were perhaps more fluid in nature like the image of Ardhanarishwara. There are passages in the Kama Sutra that talk about same-sex love. These things are still there on the surface within Indian culture but the colonised mind has been conditioned to think that they are not. I believe what has been happening is that we have been thinking along those lines and that is why there is such a disparity between mythology, the old world, and the new world.

In 2012, my grandfather died. It was a very difficult time for me. We went to India with his ashes and there were many people who came to pay their respects. I did not have any space. To get out one day, I went to the market and I picked up the Shrimad Bhagvad Gita. I thought that I would sit there and read it. I had always been interested in doing it, but never had the time. I believed it would be my salvation. And, boy, was it my salvation! Reading it, I began to understand the spiritual higher plane beyond the ritualistic Hinduism that we know today. Consequently, whenever I go to India (which I try to do yearly), I sit and read the text from start to finish. I do not see it as a religious text; I see it as a universal bounty of knowledge. The book does not teach about a specific religion. It is the book of life. It relates to you every time you read it in regards to what is going on in your life and how you are navigating any struggles that you may have. Since that point, the Shrimad Bhagvad Gita has been one of the fundamental stabilities that I have had, allowing me to become stronger and have the courage of conviction to be myself even more confidently.

My grandfather's passing led me to become more synched with my religion, to understand it more. At the same time, something was always calling me back to South Asian dance narratives. In 2013, this led me to realise that I wanted dance to be my career and decide to come out of what I call my 'retirement'. I began probing South Asian dance and the possibilities of the work that I could create through that. Even though I had not gone through the formal training, I could see and understand things that other people could not. I began to revisit and further my experimentation with surface level techniques, with movements, and aesthetics, questioning what they meant to me. After a period of community classes, I decided to go further and undertake formal training in kathak with Nahid Siddiqui, a global exponent of kathak, at the Midlands Art Centre. All of this has pushed me to work with a production house to mount my show YAATRA. Nahid and I spent an intensive four weeks together in the studio working on the piece in which she pushed me to open myself up as a person. I had been hiding. I was claiming that I was okay but I was wrestling with the personal struggles that I had with acceptance, with people's reactions to me and with their unconscious bias about my being gay. As part of this, she taught me a kathak piece that focuses on a Nayika, who sees Krishna for the first time and falls in love with him. She challenged me to imagine that I was seeing Krishna and really feeling those emotions.

YAATRA is a bill of kathak and contemporary dance that explores the rich possibilities rooted in LGBT+ narratives. Faith and identity are interleaved within the Indian mythology. It raises the question: What does dance look like through a South Asian queer lens? We live our life around the circle of faith, it is intertwined with our lives and with our culture. Often people get culture and religion confused and I can understand that fully because there is a very fine line between the two. As a British Asian, I have learnt to navigate between what are society's rules and what the religious guidance is around how you should behave as a Hindu. For me, I really hope that this means the show connects with somebody else who identifies as being LGBT+, to make them know that they are not alone in the world out there. It is also about exposing a side of sexuality within an ethnic culture that people may not know about as these narratives are very underrepresented and underexposed.

The first piece of YAATRA, *Awakening*, is in two sections and expresses my journey from a Vaishnava tradition into a Shaivite tradition, which is much more spiritualistic, meditative, and yoga-based. *Awakening* looks at my present and into my past. The first section explores the relationship with Shiva and Parvati, looking at the gender binaries and the fluidity I see within myself. Although I identify as a gay man, I do not want to be categorised as having the stereotypical traits of a man. Though I do not identify as transgender, I see that fluidity within myself and this section explores a balance of masculinity and femininity together. That is the whole idea of the Shiva and Parvati union. They are yin and yang, the masculine and the feminine as one being. Shiva is not without Parvati, Parvati is not without Shiva, that is why she is called Adhya-Shakti and he is called Adhi-Yogi. The powerful image of them together as half-man, half-woman is Ardhanarishwara. What baffles me is that this image is so religiously revered within a mythical and ritualistic context, but is not on people's radars within the context of contemporary society.

The second part of *Awakening* uses kathak to challenge the classical form of gender. By classical, I do not mean classical dance, I mean the classical, utopian, idealistic view of gender. I explore a piece where Nayika looks at Krishna for the first time and they fall in love. What does it mean when it is a man portraying that? What does it look like when a man falls in love with his male guard? What gender do you see? I am interested in playing with that. In the kathak tradition, which is a storytelling art, a man would take on the role of a woman and vice versa, so it was a very gendered story. I am interested to see how that looks as a gay man. The set uses ten or eleven temple bells exploring what it looks like when this piece is imagined in a temple. How does that fit in with people's perceptions and the limits of their comfort? At the same time, what does it look like when a gay man is creating a temple and a faith space for themself anywhere? Spirituality teaches us that we do not necessarily need human forms of idols or deities — Shiva himself is represented by a rock. It is about having God within all of us. YAATRA really expresses how I have navigated all these intersectionalities as a British Asian.

The second section of YAATRA is a contemporary dance piece also known as *Yaatra* that fundamentally explores my present and where I currently fit in relation to ritualistic worship and spiritual practice in my faith. Yaatra can mean a physical and spiritual journey and that is really important. *Yaatra* questions the image of a gay man in society and advocates for that voice. The temple bells stay in place throughout the production as this piece too discusses religious space, as well as what it looks like for the performer to create a space for themself, alongside the relationship between my faith and my dance. I make connections with my faith using prayer beads and ghungaroos. Within my practice, I use 108 ghungaroos on each foot and 108 on the mala. 108 is a very auspicious number for Hindus, so that relationship is interdependent. It allows me to feel more control about how I worship. It is not just about bowing your head in front of an idol.

The process of putting together YAATRA has allowed me to think of myself and my faith differently. The past is important but you should not let it define you. I have always been lucky that I have had the strength to continue despite adversity. I do not want to be the spokesperson for the entire LGBT+ South Asian community, but I feel it is important to have my voice heard. Moving forward, I want to further explore what the South Asian body looks like in dance. Should it be deemed as political then so be it. Much of YAATRA is inspired by my dual heritage as British Asian who identifies as being homosexual. For example, in response to the decriminalisation of homosexuality in India, Mandeep Raikhy choreographed *Queen Size*, a piece about the imposition of the eye into a gay man's private sex life, totally turning the voyeuristic viewpoint around. I think if artists in India can do that amidst the potential of criminal ramifications, then I have to count my blessings. In the UK, there are no laws about being openly gay. I am free to be, so I want to be as proactive as I can in whichever way that I can.

Isabella Segal (photo: Ben Katzler)

In My DNA

Isabella Segal

I have an unshakeable belief in God. Being born into the Jewish religion is my route to God. Judaism a very structured religion that I try and live my life by. I like the Jewish way of life. I like the culture, the traditions, and the strong family values. We are a small community within the UK, just over 250,000. That is fewer than New York City, which has over 1,000,000 Jews. We are a diminishing community, so to me it's important that my children, if possible, marry within the religion. That way we regenerate the religion. My son married a Jewish girl last year and my grandson is Jewish. Under Jewish law the child will follow its mother's religion. I like Jewish food and the way of cooking and the rituals. Jewish Sabbath (Shabbat) is Friday night into Saturday, and whilst I'm not observant of Shabbat to the letter, it's nice on Friday evening that we'll go home and light candles to welcome in the Shabbat bride and we will have a family meal — a traditional chicken soup and roast chicken. It's all very comforting. It makes me feel good and I want my kids and grandson to be part of that. Foodwise, I do not eat anything from the pig. To be kosher, Jewish food has to come from an animal which chews the cud and has a cloven hoof and is killed in a particular way called shechita. So pig isn't kosher, but cow and giraffe are. As well as eating kosher meat, I separate meat and milk at home though I don't have a separate sink for each. There are different rules for different things and I think you find your own boundaries, tailoring the religion to your requirements.

The main Jewish holidays are Rosh Hashanah, the two days of New Year, and Yom Kippur, the Day of Atonement ten days later. I observe them. Those are good days for me. You can look forward to the holidays because they mark the year. When it's Rosh Hashanah, I know it's a family event and it will be a happy time. It's therapeutic because as an accountant I'm a problem-solver giving out advice. To sit in the synagogue for two or three hours without questions is great. The service I go to is in Hebrew and while I couldn't give you a direct translation of the prayers, I have heard them for many, many years and so it is very comforting. I go to the synagogue and fast on the Day of Atonement. It's cleansing.

My transition within the religion has not been straightforward, however. There are three main branches of Judaism: the modern Liberal

43

or Reform arm, the ultra-orthodox arm, and the Conservative or United Synagogue arm, which is where I fit in. Whereas Liberal Judaism is more user-friendly (you can drive on the Sabbath and the service is partly in English), United Synagogue Judaism is more traditional: prayers are in Hebrew, men and women are separated in the synagogue, women sit behind a curtain or in their own section, and so on (though, even if apparently the men preside over the service, it seems to me that the women are running things behind the scenes, albeit in a very clever way!). The issues I have had come back to Leviticus 18. This passage says homosexuality is an abomination as a man should not waste his seed, but it is sometimes also translated to talk about not wearing clothes of the opposite gender. When I first decided to transition, I was concerned that I would lose my Jewish identity. I felt that the United Synagogue may not be accepting of me, but I wanted to remain a member because we have our own cemeteries which are only available to members. My family are buried there too. To help with this, for about a year before I transitioned, I would go to Beit Klal Yisrael (BKY), a Liberal synagogue in London. At the time there was a rabbi there called Judith who was incredibly supportive of me. I never felt at home within Liberal and Reform Judaism — it was too modern and I wasn't used to it — but BKY made me realise I would not lose my Jewish identity.

My younger sister was diagnosed with terminal cancer in 2011 and when you lose someone dear to you there's a greater being that helps you through that loss. For me that was faith. It was believing that there is something beyond living on this earth. I don't know what that is, but I think it's a good thing. When my sister was dying, I knew that I had to go back to the United Synagogue, so I went to see the rabbi where I belonged, a very nice chap, and we had a long chat — to his credit, we went for a meal together and he had no problem with seeing me dress female. I explained the situation about my sister and he said that I could come back, however it might be difficult for people there to accept me as female as they had known me before, and perhaps I should consider joining another United Synagogue congregation. At the time, I went away and thought about it, and realised I could take it one of two ways. Either it was an easy fix for him to send me away (solving a potential problem for him) or it was genuinely the right thing to say. I think it was the latter, so I went to another local synagogue where the rabbi is ultra-orthodox Lubavitch. The community was incredibly supportive and protective, making me feel very welcome, particularly certain women who were great allies. The rabbi can be difficult, but difficulty is part of the trans journey.

My sister passed away about a week after I joined my new synagogue. When a blood relative passes away, in Judaism there is a period called the shiva when close relatives mourn for seven days. Within this time, there is a powerful prayer you say called the Kaddish, an incredible prayer that you say if you have lost a close blood relative. There is a debate in the Jewish community about the Kaddish and whether women should be allowed to say the prayer. An edict came out from the Chief Rabbi to say that women may, so I went to the synagogue to say the Kaddish. Each time I was saying it, however, there was a man in the male part of the synagogue who had the most booming voice and was completely drowning me out. I knew that he wasn't in mourning and wasn't sure why he was saying this prayer, so I asked him. He said that he was saying it for the six million Jewish people who perished in the holocaust and all those who had no-one to say Kaddish for them. My response was that I respect that, but I'm actually praying for a blood relative, asking him to speak softer so that I could concentrate on my prayer. I didn't get anywhere. Was it deliberate? The rabbi would say it wasn't, but I found the whole thing disappointing.

My sister didn't know about my transition. I began transitioning at Charing Cross gender clinic in May 2012. She had a major series of seizures in February 2013. I had told Charing Cross that I was going to transition full-time that same month, but I decided to delay. It was only a matter of time and I didn't want to burden my sister. The clinic was great about it. In the end, I transitioned in May because I got outed at work (which was probably the best thing for me). When I went to see my sister I was androgynous, however I do wonder how she would have dealt with it because as a child, there were signs. I was born in 1956, my dad was a black cab driver and my mum was the matriarch in the home. I knew from the age of four that I should be a girl, but in the late 1950s and early 1960s we weren't where we are now. I was a bright little kid and I knew that I wasn't living in the right gender. From the age of about eight or nine I would cross-dress secretly, because I couldn't explain what was going on. I had my first bout of clinical depression at the age of twelve brought on by a bullying PE teacher. I went to a very macho all-boys grammar school. It wasn't a very pleasant environment, so I used to bunk off school on a Wednesday afternoon when it was double rugby and go home to dress female. It was the early 1970s, Rod Stewart and David Bowie — great years. I had long hair and would get dressed and be the girl I wanted to be. One day my sister came home and caught me. I begged her not to tell my parents but she did. We sat down and had a conversation, which was pretty good. They told me if it was a problem we could get some help. Maybe it was the best or worst decision of my life, but I managed to talk my way out of it and went straight back into the closet, dressing secretly.

When I went through puberty, I wanted to go out with girls but also be the girl. It was confusing. There was peer pressure too. All your friends are going out with girls so you overcompensate and hide your inner feelings because you don't want people to know. I met my wife when I was twenty-one. Lovely girl, easy person to live with, attractive. I thought if I got married the trans might go away. It did for about six months, but it came back. I told my wife about the cross-dressing about three or four years into the marriage and she was not too bad about it, provided it was private. At least I didn't have to dress on my own, but I did feel self-conscious. Due to this, and alongside many other people who have been through the trans journey, my mental health became an issue. My son was born in 1985 and my daughter in 1988. At that time, I was a partner on the fast track of a very nice accounting firm with good prospects, but depression hit me again. I had to spend some time in a psychiatric hospital. I had just seized up. In 1988, companies' attitudes to mental health weren't what they are now, so I was off the fast track and couldn't get a job. Nobody wanted to employ you if you had mental health issues, so I went out and formed my own practice. We did okay. I built the practice up from just me in 1989 when we started to about twenty people in 2007, but the trans issues just don't go away. I was still secretly cross-dressing and in 2008 I had a really bad bout of clinical depression. I didn't want to be on this planet anymore. I spent three and a half months in a psychiatric hospital.

After I left the hospital and my sister was diagnosed with terminal cancer, I decided I needed to do something. I was fifty-five and you only have one life. I found a gender psychiatrist, a trans man. We didn't really get along, however, so I went to my psychiatrist at the hospital. He didn't get it, asking, 'Why didn't you tell me you are gay?' I am not gay. He might have been a good depression doctor, but he certainly didn't understand trans issues. Yet I knew I had to talk to someone. I ended up seeing a cognitive behaviour therapist privately. It took me four attempts, but when I did eventually tell her, she said 'Is that it?' This deep, dark inner secret that has haunted me! She encouraged me to start dressing female and I went to an event called Sparkle in Manchester. It was my first chance to dress female for a whole weekend. From then, I knew. I decided to transition. I started living full-time female in 2013, had gender reassignment surgery in 2015, breast augmentation surgery in 2016 and some voice surgery in 2018 (which didn't work, so I'm getting another batch soon — my biggest problem is my voice). It hasn't been the most difficult journey as far as trans issues go, but it hasn't been easy.

As I began to transition, my wife and I had a number of separations. The first was in 2015. Before I had gender reassignment surgery, we were having a difficult time. I think she felt that up until I had the surgery, there was a chance I would change my mind. There weren't any chances. In the end, we split six months before the surgery, but when I had the operation, I needed some help. It's a big operation, a three month recovery. I thought, 'I'm living on my own in this one bed flat but I have this lovely family house, I'm going to move back in.' My wife couldn't cope with helping me, and I understand why. Luckily, my mum was brilliant — Jewish mothers are incredible. She looked after me and has never criticised me once. After that, the final separation came when my mum was diagnosed with cancer and I moved in with her to help. I haven't left. I knew it was the right thing to do. Now the marriage has finished, but my wife will always be someone that I care for and I'll always be someone she cares for. Though we haven't lived together since 2017, we have been on holiday together. The intimacy has ended, we won't live together again, but we will remain friends.

Recently, the Chief Rabbi sent out a booklet addressed to Jewish schools to help to make them more LGBT-inclusive. It was incredibly moving, there was one story that reduced me to tears. However, there has also been a letter from religious leaders — Jewish, Muslim and Christian — to the Secretary of State for Education hoping to regulate and monitor teaching about LGBT identity in faith schools. I saw that the rabbi of the synagogue that I went to had signed this, so I sent him a text asking him about it. I got a very polite response basically telling me to go away. I wasn't having that. I pointed out that the Chief Rabbi had issued the booklet and asked why he hadn't adhered to it. Eventually we agreed to meet. It was bizarre because he tried to turn it all around on me, saying that the LGBT community should be more approachable for the rabbis, as well as telling me how far the Conservative rabbis had moved on LGBT matters. Subsequently, all of the rabbis withdrew their signatures anyway because some of the other signatories were quite radical and they didn't want to be associated with it, but the whole thing was absurd. Eventually, I said that I would stand up in front of the congregation and share my journey because I didn't choose to be trans and I would have done anything I could to not be trans. By transitioning I have lost an incredible marriage, friends and a house, but equally I couldn't have carried on living without being trans. I had to do this. I told him that in a synagogue of over 100 people, there must be another LGBT person apart from me. I asked how the parents of an LGBT child would handle it. I think that got through to him and I am hoping to see change. I do a lot of talking to both Jewish and non-Jewish groups about my journey. It's about education. If you can educate people they will become more tolerant.

Increasingly, as I get older, I have less confidence in the rabbis who lead our communities. Twenty years ago, I thought these were leaders of the community that I looked up to, but now I am becoming disillusioned as I have seen some of their fallibilities. I didn't realise at the time, but when I moved synagogues, there had been a management committee meeting to discuss my joining. I'm a human being. I have belonged to the United Synagogue for over thirty years and paid my annual fees. Why would you need a meeting? It was to approve that I could sit with the women and use the women's toilet. If I had known at the time, I wouldn't have moved. The rabbis even asked me when I die, who is going to wash me. Usually it is someone of the same gender. My response was, 'I don't care, I will be dead.' I don't have a Gender Recognition Certificate, but I hope that my kids know I want to be buried in my female gender and not in my birth gender. Because of this I have reined in my visits to the synagogue recently. I do go on the High Holy Days and on the anniversaries of my sister's and father's deaths to say prayers, however.

I find that I don't fit in with women or with men. Generally, I've not found the women's community to be supportive or inclusive, but I have been very welcomed by the Jewish Gay and Lesbian Group. At first, I would say, 'I'm not gay, why would I come?' but eventually I did go to a women-only event, a barbecue, and I was made to feel so welcome. Being me, of course, I had to nag the group to change their name. I told them if they wanted to attract younger people they had to stop being so dated and drop 'Gay and Lesbian'. It has to be Jewish LGBT, which they did! One of the big things that I would like to see is the Board of Deputies of British Jews (the Jewish representation group to which each synagogue nominates a member) invite an LGBT representative. We have a long way to go, which is disappointing. I lived fifty-five years in the straight world without any inkling of the issues that LGBT people have to go through. I learn all the time and we need representation so others can too. All this doesn't stop me taking comfort in my religion, however. In fact, I think that my relationship with faith comes about when I have difficult times in my life, when I am struggling. I am so proud of being Jewish. It's in my DNA. I wear a Star of David. I'm proud to wear it. I'm privileged to be born Jewish. I enjoy it, I embrace it, and I want to continue with it.

Earlier this year, I had a heart event (not quite a heart attack, but I needed a procedure). After that, you address your life. I thought, 'I'm in my early 60s, I don't want to work so hard.' I won't have another long-term partner. I can't recreate the fabulous friendship and relationship that I had. I don't want to. What I want are good friends whom I can spend time with and I care about. I'm not quite retiring, but things are changing.

Sabah Choudrey (photo: Sayf Taj)

The Things I Can't Put Into Words

Sabah Choudrey

Islam is something I was brought up with. I went to Quran school, the mosque and celebrated various Muslim holidays with family, yet for a while it didn't feel like something I was connected to. It felt like something I was forcing. I would pray and ask, 'Is this how it is meant to feel?' It just never really clicked for me. Then I figured out I wasn't straight — that I had feelings that 'were not right'. Somehow you learn from a young age that these feelings don't go with what religion is.

I remember a conversation I had with my mum while we were driving to school. I was about thirteen or fourteen and feeling emo. I told her, 'I don't believe in God.' I remember a feeling, almost like an anger that I needed to tell her. The response was, 'Yes you do, it's just a phase.' I was even more angry, I felt, 'I am trying to tell you something: I don't believe in this thing that you've forced me to think about all the time and now you are telling me it's just a phase.' From then on I was more resistant towards God because I felt everyone was pushing religion on to me and telling me how to think. I also had different things to focus on: being a teenager, coming out (at that time, as a lesbian), being rebellious, going to parties, socialising, drinking, smoking, being young, immature and carefree (or selfish, which would be more accurate). I pushed being Muslim away.

Then I went to Brighton to study and had my atheist phase. It feels so weird that I would ever say that now. There was a part of me that was still not sure that I was an atheist, I wasn't even sure that I didn't believe in a God or religion, but it became my identity. It makes me feel sad, almost, that I wanted nothing to do with Islam and religion. And I think it was influenced by people around me, a lot of white queer people who had Christian upbringings. I thought, 'That's who I want to be. That's where I fit.' Brighton is such a white city and it was more desirable to say these things because I felt like I stood out and didn't want to be the only one. Then I began learning about feminism, intersectional oppressions, institutional -isms and racisms. I realised that even though I was in a white queer community with atheist friends, I was still going to be brown, Pakistani and read as Muslim. I was still not going to have the same experiences. It was a pretty rough period. Learning about oppressions for the first time will always be heart-breaking. I saw it all around me and felt I couldn't escape how people perceive me. Then I felt that I don't have to push away one thing to be another thing. I began to understand that even Islam can sit within a structure of patriarchy and be taught within a way that fits certain models like heteronormativity and patriarchal beliefs. Why couldn't I learn about it for myself and start again? So I did.

Having finished university, I remember sitting in my room and reading *The Color Purple*. In each chapter, Celie writes prayers to God and eventually reaches a point where she wonders, 'Have you even been listening? Are you even there?' During one scene, her friend Shug reminds her in a playful way that God is all around: God is the colour purple, the trees, everything. Something about reading that caused a shift. Outside, there was a thunderstorm — dark, loud, lots of lightning. It was an electric night and I could really feel it: this is what they are talking about. Things reframed in my mind and felt different, I had an uncertainty but it didn't feel unfamiliar. I was in a place where I could think about it and begin to hold it. That night made me feel like God, Allah or religion didn't have to be something I was taught — I could redefine it for myself.

Around the same time, I went to the Inclusive Mosque Initiative which holds multifaith open prayer spaces and other events such as conferences around the diversity of Islam. It is a very feminist organisation run by really awesome people. Seeing an inclusive Muslim space where I didn't feel like I have to know everything was a relief. Going to an inclusive Jumu'ah, however, I got really nervous. I still felt I wasn't Muslim enough. I asked what I was doing and what it meant. I didn't know the prayer by heart or if I was doing it right. It threw me off. That was years ago. Those feelings are still there but I have tried to include that as part of my relationship to Islam. There will always be a space for doubt and not feeling good enough. It's an important part of my relationship to faith. I don't want to feel like I know everything, to know that everything is certain. Other parts of my identity — my gender and my sexuality — never stay the same. I want to afford the same fluidity to my religion. For some people, Islam is much more of a binary. Either you are a Muslim or not. Either you are strict or liberal. It's hard to get away from.

I have reclaimed my Islam for myself. One of the most important parts of Islam for me now is the intention behind your acts. I believe in having an honest intention — not necessarily a good intention, but a true one. Whatever I do, I at least want to be to honest with myself, to know I am not doing something just to perform. It comes down to the 'not being Muslim enough'. If your intention is honest, does it matter what you are doing to make yourself a good Muslim? 'Good' things can come with so many different intentions, but if those intentions are honest then I think that's the best you can do. To place myself within Islam, I start off with my intentions. I know that I can't always fast when asked, that I can't pray five times a day, that I can't always stick to halal things — but if I am honest with myself and know my limits, then I can begin to take little steps. When I reclaimed Islam, I felt the pressure to fast during Ramadan and it made me feel bad about myself. My motivation became to feel less bad and it began to feel really murky. It wasn't what I wanted. Being religious isn't about making yourself feel bad, guilty or ashamed. That won't help me to lead a better life. Allah knows everything anyway. Having an honest intention keeps things very personal. It makes sure that I am doing things for me, rather than to appease someone else.

Islam is the things I can't describe or put into words. Now my faith is not so much a part of me as something that is around me, something that I am in relation to. If I claimed it was a part of me, it would feel too definite. Relationships change all the time. It's something that other people are a part of too. Islam, for me, is about community, as opposed to being in a relationship with God. I feel like it is about everyone. Islam links all these people together all over the world: past, present and future. That assurance feels really powerful. When I talk about being Muslim to non-Muslims at an event, I have to position Islam in relation to what they think. Either I am putting it next to all the terrible, negative untrue stereotypes or someone will say something that brings it up. The stories and experiences I am sharing become framed for the audience. I am comfortable with that as I know what people expect to see, but I don't have much room to hold that space for myself. I don't have much room to check in and ask, 'How are we doing, Islam and I?'

My community has changed so much since I left Brighton. I moved away to care for and support my dad. Leaving a community that was very white, very queer, very feminist but quite fragile, at times, for queer people of colour. Coming home to West London, where there is not much going on, things are very chill. It's a huge Muslim area, there is a huge population of Somalis and South Asians, it's so different. I don't feel like this is my community but it made me want to find a community that looks like this, that looks more Muslim, that has more people of colour. Coming home, I wasn't sure where I stood, but I wanted to feel like this was my community too. I try to spend time with other queer Muslims and people who have different relationships to Islam so that I can see lots of different types of faith. Being with them feels different, knowing that there are people there who don't have to ask questions. So many times when I was with my friends in Brighton, I found myself explaining my culture and upbringing. Community is when you are with someone and don't need to explain. When you are like, 'Family, you know?' and the response is 'Yup!' It's the kind of people who know exactly what you mean. Community is tied to race and faith and queerness but it is not limited to that.

Graduating from university, I organised Trans Pride Brighton. It was a time when I felt the community I was part of, a little pocket of cis lesbians in Brighton, didn't fit me anymore. I went to an FTM (Female to Male) group for trans men desperate to find a community. I wanted to walk into the room and feel like people got me, to feel like I related to everyone. I just didn't. I felt more lonely. I remember looking around and everyone else was white and of different ages. The narratives of family that came up were so unrelatable because of different cultural backgrounds and the lack of presence of religion. I started to wonder if I should be prepared to push my parents away, move out, put emotional and physical distance between us. It made me more scared. I had the same feelings when Brighton Pride came around. It wasn't my Pride anymore. It didn't fit me. In a way, I had a selfish drive to carve out a space for myself, but knowing that it would help someone else.

After Pride, someone arranged a coffee meeting between a group of trans people, an LGBT police liaison officer, and someone from Brighton and Hove City Council to speak about how we were all doing as there were always transphobic incidents at Pride (and generally). Before Trans Pride Brighton, we didn't really have a community event that bonded us all together except for the Transgender Day of Remembrance, an annual national memorial day where we honour trans people who have lost their lives. Going to a service, you saw the lack of trans people of colour in that space compared to the number we were honouring. I felt like we could do more to make it feel like community — more to honour people, to protect others and to celebrate. We wanted there to be a happier, more powerful, celebratory day. There is so much to celebrate — trans people are fucking amazing.

Suddenly the conversation begun to revolve around creating our own Pride. At first I thought it was a hypothetical conversation: What if we held a march down North Street and West Street in Brighton? But then we were really talking about holding a march. I thought it was ridiculous: there was no way you were going to see a group of ten visibly trans people walking through a student, laddy area. Then it became about organising a space. Even though being visible, marching and protest are such an important part of Pride, we couldn't ensure it was safe, so creating a space felt right. It was hard — we were all trans people getting by, we didn't have lots of free time — but particular people in the community made sure it happened. It was deeply moving how many people wanted to make Trans Pride Brighton happen that year. The event was for everyone but centring the trans community. I could look at everyone there — family, friends, supporters, councillors, whatever — and see community; it was everyone who cared. It was really amazing. Quickly the event became three days: a film night on the Friday, a park event on the Saturday with a party in the evening, and a picnic on the Sunday. The event still happens every year and is growing bigger — it's becoming a thing that trans people look out for and want to go to.

Following Trans Pride Brighton, I helped organise Queer Picnic. I had moved home to London and found a queer people of colour community. Pride in London is such a climax in LGBTQ lives. It's a time to celebrate, it's summer, a lot of people have taken time off work, but a lot of queer people of colour (and especially those of faith) felt let down. We wanted something more. There was a shared feeling that Pride in London was not political anymore, even though there was so much we needed to fight for still. It didn't feel like our Pride. A few friends — all queer and trans people of colour — just got together for dinner and began talking about how crap Pride in London was and what we could do instead. This was an amazing group of people: creative, passionate, super-talented, musicians, performers, writers, makeup artists. We thought, 'Why don't we all just have a picnic and get together?'

We just wanted to centre trans and queer people of colour who have been at the front of so many Pride and LGBTQ movements — to celebrate that at an open, free, accessible event. We talked about everything. It was a really necessary dialogue. Because I had just come out of the world of organising Trans Pride Brighton on such a massive scale, I thought we had to get in touch with the park and the police. Half of the table said, 'Fuck that, we can do whatever we want, we don't need to talk to the police or get permission to do this,' a real radical, political, anarchist push. We knew that though this was the alternative Pride event, it still wasn't for everyone. There would still be differences in the community but we wanted to try and look after everyone and create as inclusive an event as we could. One of us had a sound system and we agreed to do speeches and rallies and hold it as an open event. We each took roles, first aid and so on. It felt powerful to be able to centre different people in this queer, alternative Pride event. It wasn't that hard — we argued a bit, but that was it.

The first time Queer Picnic happened, we met up at Burgess Park in London. It was really chilled. We had music on, spread out mats and labelled an area for people who were drinking and an area for children, some of us did Namaaz in a different space. It was Ramadan, so we decided to make it a sober event or at least centre sobriety. It wasn't just about Muslims, it was a family event too, and people have different relationships to alcohol and sobriety. A few hours where we just hung out. We timed it so it was just after the Pride march ended (or when it was meant to end, it never ends on time) and quite nearby so that people could come to both. We had discussed that some people would want to go to Pride as well and that's okay. It was just about having a different space, it was never about being instead of or a competition. There just needs to be more spaces. On the event we had a political message saying that we were centring people of colour, don't be racist, think about your whiteness or your cisness, think about how much space you are taking up, remember who the event is for. We invited our friends thinking it would be a very small get together but suddenly there were 2,000 people attending.

I kept having conversations with people online or at events and realising that there are so many of us — queer Muslims, trans Muslims, queer desi people, trans people of colour. Often I felt like a matchmaker — linking up friends who have similar experiences or are from similar backgrounds — so recently a friend and I set up DesiQ, a group for queer desi people in London. There's no aim. We just wanted to create a place where people could meet and not feel alone. Even if people didn't want to hang out again, they knew that the space existed, that they all existed and were still here. We established the group thinking, 'Well, there are at least two of us who wanted to be involved,' but people started joining. I want to continue creating spaces which don't have to exist for a purpose except that people who feel like they fall under loose definitions, or can benefit from the space and don't like those definitions, can exist.

Sometimes I don't think of myself as an activist. A little while ago, a friend said the phrase 'the reluctant activist' and I can really relate to that. As someone who announces their identity on a platform, everything I do is suddenly marked as activism for that identity or that community. I want there to be more spaces for people. I want to interrogate why there aren't. I want to interrogate myself and why I can speak about certain things. Why can I talk about these issues? Why are these issues only talked about by people who look like me? I think about myself differently now. I see the privileges I do have. I can be an out trans person because I am masculine and pass as a man sometimes. I'm able-bodied. I want to keep doing and keep creating, even if right now I am not doing as much as I was. Where I can, I will. I am still writing, still thinking, still having conversations with my friends. It might not be on such a huge scale, but I am still working. I want to look after my community, because community will look after me too.

Path of Many Journeys

Selina Khunkhuna

Sikhism wasn't a conscious choice, it was something I was born into. I was raised in a traditional Sikh family. My mum and dad had an arranged marriage, which was typical for their generation. My dad was born in India and came over when he was twenty-one to marry my mum, who was born in Nottingham and nineteen at the time. In Sikhism, like other Asian religions, there are many castes. Our caste is Jat, the landowners. As a child my faith meant things like trips to the temple or the Five Ks, one of which is to not cut your hair. I was quite young when my mum decided to cut her hair short and I remember this being a big deal in the family, especially with my dad's sisters who are more traditional. My mum's mum, my Nani, was the most religious person I was around. She would go not just to the gurdwara but also the Hindu temple, the mandir, and believed in various superstitions: not washing your hair on certain days, not eating meat on certain days, eating sugar if you sneezed once before you left the house. Yet all these things happened in the background. They were related to my religion but it's only looking back as an adult that I can see how faith was always part of my life. I didn't know any different.

I grew up in a community that was predominantly white, so I went to a school without any other Sikh children. There were a couple of other Asian kids, a Hindu boy in my year, but other than that it was a very white culture, meaning I never thought about my faith until later in life. I remember my aunt coming to visit and picking me up from school with her sons who had traditional long hair and were wearing the kurti. I remember being awfully embarrassed. I didn't identify with that part of the culture. I didn't feel that I wanted to share that part of my life with my peers because it made me different. I didn't talk with friends at school about faith or how we celebrated the Sikh culture. I was always very shy and quiet. I was slightly more confident in Religious Education at secondary school but even then, when asked to do a talk in front of the class, I didn't. Though there wasn't any open prejudice, I just didn't feel like an expert and didn't want to see myself as different to everyone I was surrounded by at school.

I was always a late bloomer when it came to relationships. At school, my peers didn't see me as approachable. I was very quiet and people probably thought that I wasn't supposed to date white people, being Asian. I had a crush on one of my female teachers but didn't think too much about it. At college I wasn't supposed to go to parties, I had quite an overprotective mother so there wasn't much opportunity to date. My journey was slow-burning. It wasn't until I went to university that I began to develop feelings for the same sex and the opposite sex: moving away from home was my opportunity to explore relationships. In my first year I lived with a Sikh girl. We developed a close bond very quickly and she became my best friend. It was a very intense friendship, we spent a lot of time together and things soon developed into a relationship. Though it was non-sexual — she had boyfriends and I was still very shy — she was my first kiss on a night out. Things came to a head when my feelings became so intense that I couldn't deal with it. I didn't know how to tell her so I had a breakdown and suffered with depression. I took a year out of university and was sectioned when I was twenty-one, just after my birthday. It had all spiralled into this intense infatuation with someone who I couldn't be with and couldn't tell. I didn't know what was going on with me. Afterwards, the psychiatrist said that it was the social implications of that relationship that caused that breakdown. Having feelings for my best friend, another woman and a Sikh, was massive.

My family didn't understand what was going on. We had never come across mental health problems before so my mum, her brothers and my Nani started turning to spiritual things to try and help. A Hindu priest who claimed to be a doctor came to the house, gave me a card and began asking if I had a Muslim boyfriend. In our community a Sikh and a Muslim having a relationship is frowned upon so they assumed I had gone to Manchester for university, met a Muslim boy and had a dilemma. Little did they know it was a Sikh girl! It wasn't a nice experience. I wasn't comfortable with all of the superstitious things that I was asked to do because I didn't understand them. I had gone from having an independent life at Manchester with friends to being at home again, sectioned, and all of a sudden being asked to chuck a coconut in the river because it was supposed to help. There was a lot of anger about that for a few years, but I understand now that was my family's way of helping because they just didn't know what to do.

From the experience with this particular girl, I realised that I wasn't straight. The first person I told was my mum. I said to her that I was bisexual, that I was attracted to a girl, that I had fallen in love and wanted to marry her. Then I told a flatmate at university and slowly but surely started to tell more friends. Some were okay about it, some weren't, I lost some along the way but that was part of my journey. At the same time I began a Masters at university because I wanted to make good out of all the bad experiences I had in Manchester, but I had a second breakdown. At twenty-two, I reached a turning point. I was wondering if I would have the traditional Sikh marriage to a man and had become involved with someone who seemed to tick all the boxes but when it came to crunch time, I realised that wasn't what I wanted to do. I fell into a spiral and had another episode of depression.

After university, I moved back to Nottingham and started working for the NHS. For the first time I met LGBT people who were open and comfortable with who they were. Of course, I probably had come across LGBT people at university but I didn't know — I didn't make the most of Canal Street unfortunately! Because of this I felt that I could talk about my sexuality, that I could make friends with these people and go clubbing with them. I felt that — Yes! — this was my foot in. I was twenty-four. From then on I started to go out to gay places, I felt more comfortable about my sexuality and met my first girlfriend. It was a positive journey with my sexuality, until I reached my late twenties. I hit the age that marriage began being talked about again. All of my cousins were getting married and I started to think, 'What about me?' This let to my third and final episode with depression.

When I think of community I think of pressure. In the LGBT community, people often don't believe in bisexuality, so trying to fit in and be accepted is difficult. Usually this comes from lesbians who tell me that I need to admit that I am also a lesbian, which is a myth and can be hard. I also feel the pressure of the Asian community, both from those of the same and of different religions. I feel there is an unsaid pressure, that there are expectations about what people in our community do. Community is a pressure for me. Tradition is similar. Tradition is about abiding by certain stipulations: it's traditional to get married, it's traditional to go to the temple, it's traditional to not drink, not to eat meat, not to cut your hair, not to have sex before marriage. For a long time I assumed that if I did not get married by a certain age then people would wonder what was wrong with me. I didn't feel comfortable going to the gurdwara because I wanted to avoid those sort of questions; I didn't attend weddings unless I was really close with the person — not for myself, but because I didn't want my parents to be questioned about why their daughter wasn't married.

The last person I was scared to come out to was my dad. My dad has been my rock, my role model, my strength. When I had my first breakdown he took ten weeks off to look after me (and you know Indians and work — we don't take time off!). He has always been there. He is such an amazing, generous, kind, hard-working man. I do not want to portray him as some kind of godly figure but as a father he has been fantastic. His opinion matters to me more than anyone. I was twenty-eight when I came out and my dad was amazing. He was upset that I felt I couldn't confide in him earlier; he said he already knew and wondered how I ever thought he would disown me. As soon as I was accepted by him, I didn't care about anything else — no one could touch me. It gave me a second life. My twenties were hard because of my breakdowns but knowing that my dad was there to protect me from anyone and anything made me feel so lucky. Coming out to my family, there has yet to be one negative (though there have been some embarrassing times!). I know that people love me. When you are a person of faith, people think it must have been really difficult coming out to your parents. It was difficult for me because I was struggling with myself, but it wasn't difficult because of my faith. It was the opposite, a really positive experience and I became more comfortable with talking about my sexuality. In fact, I was so confident that I took part in a video campaign for Stonewall, who were looking for people from minorities to come forward and share their stories. Talking about my journey helped me process what was going on but also allowed me to understand that there was no stigma and that I didn't have to hide anymore.

My understanding of my faith is something I am still on a journey with and learning about. I recently travelled to India for the second time. When I first went as an eighteen-year-old, I didn't appreciate it. This time, travelling with my dad as a thirty-five-year-old was really meaningful. It was emotional. I didn't anticipate the trip being as meaningful as it was for me. My grandma had passed away but my dad's brother still lives there with his family and we stayed there with him on the farm in Punjab. It was significant going with my dad to learn about my history. Hearing his stories about how he grew up, what his parents went through, and where he would like his ashes scattered was really meaningful. As well as visiting the Golden Temple, I went to Anandpur, to the Sikh museum. It fascinated me. I felt so calm, so at peace, so comfortable. Even though I was dressed in Western clothes with my head covered, I just felt like I was at home. I felt so safe.

Visiting one of the local gurdwaras near the family home was particularly emotional. I burst into tears. It was like something overcame me. It was like my grandma had come back. I was swept with guilt for not having visited more. As I was sitting there, crying, I started thinking about two of my aunties who have both been role models for me in my LGBT journey. One of them married a Muslim guy and the other an English guy, both outside of the community. Each of these aunties has supported me most when I have struggled with my sexuality and with feeling comfortable in my community. I was crying in the gurdwara thinking about what they had to go through and how it has made it easier for my generation. They have taken all the crap for going against tradition but, because of what they sacrificed, I can live my life and do what I want. India just felt like home. It was a turning point. I finally felt as if I had accepted myself.

That trip made me want to embrace my religion and culture more, to not be ashamed or afraid even though I am bisexual and not doing the traditional thing. As part of this, I bought a translation of the Guru Granth Sahib, the Sikh holy book which is written in poetry. It's four huge volumes, thousands and thousands of pages, but I have been told it has the answer to every question I might have in life within it. I know that I have that now for life. I can embrace that if I want to pray, to learn more about the religion, or to discover more about myself. It is something that I want to explore and identify with now. Though I don't visit the temple often, I know that if I want to I can when it is quiet and I know that I can pray from home. Whereas before I had never shown an interest in the religion, as I grow older faith is something I can believe in and identify with, something I can relate to my upbringing and my family. My auntie who married her Muslim partner has gone through a similar journey, exploring the Sikh religion in later life and becoming more involved with the temple in America where she lives. This journey is part of me accepting who I am, accepting that I am still Sikh even though I am bisexual.

As I grow and accept myself as Sikh and as bisexual, I understand that the assumptions I have about the community are probably just fears: fears of being judged, fears of being pushed away, fears of being rejected. The reality is that I still get invited to the temple, I still get invited to weddings. No one asks my parents about when I am getting married because times have changed and people don't mither on about each other's business. People who genuinely care about me are not bothered about these things. A lot of the people I see at functions already know about my sexuality anyway, because I have been so open about it. As well as this, there are so many positives about the community: family, not leaving people on their own, looking after our elders, not letting people come to your home without feeding them. We celebrate so many wonderful events too and not just our own, but those we share with the Hindu calendar. Recently we celebrated one of my favourite days in the Sikh calendar, Raksha Bandhan, a brother-sister day. A girl will go to her brother or male cousins and tie a piece of string known as a Rakhri around their arm and give them a sweet. In return, they receive a gift and it is a celebration of the bond between brothers and sisters. It's a day where you dash around visiting all of your family and do this lovely thing to celebrate your relationships. It's about not leaving people on their own, about loving people and being together as a family, about making people feel safe and warm and welcome. I think these events are really special and I want to be a part of them. This is part of my identity and something I want to share.

Sikhism is about equality for all. As much as it gave comfort to my family at the time, superstitions are not what Sikhism is about. It is why I wanted to get the Guru Granth Sahib, so that I could interpret it for myself and not assume that certain things were part of my religion when they are not. If you look at true Sikhism it is about equality between men and women, that is what Guru Nanak wanted. Why would I not want to practice a faith that is so forward-thinking and brilliant? We have an impression of India being backwards, but in my family's local village they have a system where the mayor would be a man, then a woman, then someone from one caste and then another, just to make sure there is representation for all. Each of these things that I learnt in India made me realise that my religion is something great. I am lucky to be Sikh. I need to be proud to be Sikh. It's okay to be bisexual and to be Sikh. Now I have dreams of being the first bisexual to have a Sikh wedding in a temple. Why not? Why can't these things happen? I picture myself at my wedding, whether it is to a man or a woman, whether it is at a temple or not, wearing the traditional red. My wedding will have the beautiful traditions that I have grown up with because that is part of who I am. I do not have to lose that because I am now part of the LGBT community.

If I had not been through my journey and had to understand my sexuality, I would not have needed solace as much as I have done, I wouldn't have sought answers to questions about who I am, I wouldn't have looked for reassurance from my faith as much as I have. I have used my faith as a comfort. I have used it as a safe place. Everyone struggles with identity in different ways but for the LGBT community in particular, having confidence in who you are is fundamental and faith can really help with that.

Discovering God is still a part of my journey as I read the Guru Granth Sahib. I don't really understand who God is or what they represent. When you go to the gurdwara growing up, you identify with pictures of the Gurus and how they fought to protect the religion. Thinking about God hasn't been at the forefront of my faith. So far my faith has been about my identity and feeling a part of my family. Yet as I think about it now as I read the holy book, I believe there is something that created us, that there is something that protects us in dark times, I believe there is something that affects our destiny, I believe in things like karma, and I believe all of that comes from God. I am still on the journey of understanding my relationship with God and how important that relationship is. I see it with fresh eyes. I am taking the time to learn and educate myself because I want to and I am interested.

I want to go back to India. I want to read the Guru Granth Sahib. I want to find out more about my religion and identity. I want to celebrate my family. I want to go on that journey. I believe it will be positive and I am going to embrace it. Finally I recognise that I am still Sikh, I am still that same girl I was growing up. Meeting people who are Sikh and have homophobic views, you might believe that Sikhism is homophobic, but that is just someone's warped interpretation of the religion, not what the religion is about. I know that Sikhism wouldn't discriminate against people who are gay, bisexual or transgender, wouldn't discriminate against classes or castes, wouldn't discriminate against anything. It is not part of what the Sikh religion was originally about. Travelling to India and reading about the history of Sikhism, I know that I am supported in being a woman, in being brown, in being bisexual. No one is inferior, we are all equal. I have always known that but, after the journey I have been on, I now know how important and significant that is for me.

Mr Ekow

No Man's Land

Mr Ekow

Caught between the Rock and a hard place
Feels like I lose no matter what I choose
I've tried and tried
I've cried and cried
I've lost my mind

I was brought up going to church. Me, mum and dad, older brother, younger sister. It was a normal thing. Christianity was my identity. When I was really young, we went to a Baptist church, but at eleven we moved to an interdenominational church based around the Charismatic tradition. As a child, I had moments where Christianity wasn't something I particularly wanted to be involved with. I was a usual kid, I wanted to stay at home and watch Pokémon, rather than go to church. My mum would call me to wake up and I would pretend to be asleep. Classic behaviour. I finished children's church at eleven and stopped attending the youth group. For a while, I felt like my Christian identity wasn't as important. I wondered if I should drop it.

A shift came when I went to secondary school. I had Christian friends, but we just got on with the kinds of things kids do, being naughty or whatever. A lot of us had siblings in Year 11 and the first week of school, they came over to us and said: 'What you guys on? You gotta get your tings, yeah'. I had no idea what that meant, but it became the mission for a while — teenage boys, running around, chasing girls, getting into beef. As I became a teenager, however, I was really impacted by going away to youth weeks, seeing God move in different ways: people praying for each other, being healed by prayer, or just having a genuine sense of being towards the Word. At that point I committed my life to God. My teens became split between normal kid things and devotion — going to church, praying, reading the Bible. I began to find enjoyment in church and reclaimed it for myself.

Being touched by the power of God is hard to explain, and hard to explain away. Even as I say it now, there is a part of me that wonders what that actually means. What did people experience at those youth retreats? Was it just hype? Was it a frenzy? Was it just people saying they could feel God when they actually didn't? Though I have these questions, there has always been a significant enough proportion for me to think, 'That's some real shit there, I can't ignore that.' Church offered me time to know God personally and the chance to be in a community. It made it very easy to be Christian, having all these people like you, having a good time, doing stupid stuff, but believing the same thing. It was never awkward. In my entire childhood, I never felt ostracised because of my faith. There was never the question of 'Is God real?' amongst my friends, it was a question of 'How real do you want to take this?' It was a little bubble.

At the same time, I began to have feelings for guys when I was around twelve. No one had told me not to be gay, but it must have filtered through church and my family (who are from Ghana, where homosexuality is still culturally unacceptable). I kept things a secret and hoped it was a phase. Growing up in Croydon, there was a huge stigma. I remember having conversations with friends in the playground, asking what we would do if we found out our brother was gay. I was internally screaming, but would say things like, 'I would bang him in the face!' I hoped it would pass, but it didn't, so at fifteen I approached a member of my church. I was in tears as I explained. He asked me what I wanted to do and, with his guidance, we decided to pray about it. Although I have regrets, I am thankful that it wasn't a 'pray the demon away' kind of thing. Instead, my mentoring became based on discipleship and becoming closer to God. Not that things were easy. At the next youth retreat I attended, I became overexcited. During the evening people gave testimonies and I stood up to tell everyone that I had been gay, but no longer was. After this, a fair few people in my church knew and I began to tell some friends, positioning my sexuality as if it were a thing of the past. From then on it was a constant struggle: to not think about guys, to not look at guys, to not look at porn.

Ironically, and though I would never recommend it, in one sense it helped me to become closer to God. I felt that I couldn't get through the situation by myself so my relationship to God became a lot more intimate. I would cry with him (or her), get angry with him (or her), and try to press on with what God wanted me to be. I spent a lot of time praying. I would disappear into the room of my older brother who had left for university and spend hours praying, reading the Bible, singing praise and worship. Looking back now, a lot of it was genuine — I felt closer to God and gained a deeper understanding of the scripture — but it was coated with rejection. I was distressed. I would have wet dreams

68

about guys and wonder what I could do, I was tempted even while I was asleep. It's a strange one. I don't know if I would still be a Christian if it wasn't for those years, but I resent it at the same time.

> I remember early days, thinking it's a phase, but it never changed
> So I thought I could pray it away
> But it remained, even though I claimed
> With faith strained it weren't reality
> Struggling to maintain my sanity

Going to university, I had the bubble poked. It was a good thing. Everyone should have that experience at some point. I started studying Management and Accounting at UEA, but quickly switched to Film and Philosophy. In my second year, I began lurking on dating apps, and even almost hooked up with someone. During the lead-up I felt distraught, like it was something that I had to do. When it fell through I became super low. I thought about self-harm. I called my mentor at church in tears and he helped me through it. I opened up to a couple of guys at the Christian Union, who didn't know what to do but offered to pray with me. So the narrative of reject, reject, reject continued.

After I finished university I met a woman at church. I thought we had a lot in common, seemed to be in similar circles and that she was a good-looking girl. I thought that maybe she was the one. Before we got together, I was worried about whether it would work out. I really wanted a sign from God. Nothing came. I decided to go for it anyway. We were together for just under a year, but unfortunately I ended up messing around with another guy. I wanted to break up and move on. Again, I turned to my mentor. He suggested that I should confide in her, as it was better to be honest. She was understanding but we split up. After we parted I felt terrible for months, telling myself that I was shit and that everyone knew it. I became paranoid. I felt like what I had done was written on my face. It was awful. It was the lowest I had ever been in my life. I was in a period of nothingness. I was a youth worker at the time and I remember being at a session where all the kids were running around and I was sat there, completely dazed. Praying with my mentor, I decided to be celibate. I had hoped it was a phase, tried to change, even hoped to find the right girl. That decision lasted for about a month. Not that I did anything, but my mindset swiftly changed. I realised I couldn't do it.

At that point, I stepped away from God for about a year. I didn't want a relationship I had to keep breaking away from, feeling the pain of falling short and repenting. I saw how much that loop was starting to harm me. Repentance began to mean less yet hurt more. I would try and get closer to God, but I felt like nothing was working. I would have tears in my eyes on the way to work. I still went to church and went through the motions, but it was the most distant that I had ever felt. I was critical, but too scared to walk away, scared of how friends and family would react.

As time went on, I started to meet up with guys in secret. This brought on another low. I was worried someone would see me. A friend recognised that I was struggling and recommended that I went to see a therapist. I remember calling their office and not even being able to speak the words, but I eventually began to go. It was an interesting process. There were moments where I felt like someone had punched me in the face. After one session, I felt so fragile that I decided to get fucked up that night with some friends. Before we left the house I told a friend where I had been that day and he put two and two together. As we were walking down the road early in the morning after the night had finished, he said, 'I know.' I tried to deflect it, told him to shut up, but eventually I confided in him. The next morning I woke up with a crazy hangover and begun wondering what I was going to do. I knew that I had to come out. It just made sense. I said to God, 'I don't know if you are in this or not, but this is my only option.' That weekend, I felt that everything was swirling around me, like a tornado was pulling up deep roots and structures while I sat at the eye of the storm. I came out to a few friends first and then geared up to tell my parents. My dad surprised me and told me that people should do what they want to do. He had not been to church since I was ten and I have a cousin who is gay. I think that helped. My mother, however, is the spiritual matriarch. I could tell she was upset, but she came round, letting me know that she still loved me. I felt affirmed.

> Crying out for God to come mend me
> Cos why even make me?
> Why even take me on this journey with you?

I was out, but I didn't know if I could be a Christian and gay at the same time. I began researching, reading and watching videos. Eventually, I went to Oasis Church in London, who have a group for LGBTQ people. There I was referred to group therapy for gay Christian men run by a psychiatrist and a priest, who worked together. They helped me to rework my theological foundations. My Christianity has changed, my faith is a lot simpler, but I am happy. I am trying to love God as much as I can, love others as much as I can, and move forward. It's working for me. I am at a point where I think that God loves gay people. And this isn't to say, 'God loves gay people, but he hates their sin.' God loves gay people. I have a partner now, and we often talk about religion. He wasn't raised with faith, so we can have conversations that are free of all the politics. We educate each other and question each other.

I have been making music since I was about fourteen. When I was a kid, everyone had eight bars that they could rap. I grew up on Dizzee Rascal, Andre 3000, Nas, Mos Def. There was a strong Christian hip-hop and grime scene in London: Guvna B, Triple O, Faith Child, Dwayne Tryumf. I wanted to be a part of it. At church, I started a hip-hop group with friends; some of the music was garbage, but it was fun. We eventually parted but while I was at university I deepened my interest. I had fallen in love with art again: music, film, theatre. I realised how art speaks ideology into the world. Great art allows people to question their worldview, it asks more questions than it answers. Take *The Matrix*. Everyone watched it when I was a kid, the allegory challenged people, sometimes more than someone standing and preaching in church. That has always been what I want to achieve with my music. A lot of the time, I enjoy being in bars and clubs more than faith spaces. I want to challenge myself to do more than simply tell people to come to God. It's why I love hip-hop and folk, the music manages to be so purposive. Especially folk, which can use a lot less words because you don't have to fill the bars — you can leave empty space. I love Sufjan Stevens, Fleet Foxes, Bon Iver. Rather than dot the Is and cross the Ts, I want to make sure that I write in a way that speaks honestly from my point of view. If I can do that, anything that is important to me will seep through anyway.

Art is like looking at a beautiful starry night. If you try and take a photo of it, you will never capture exactly what you can see. Art is presenting what you are feeling. It is more than just telling them what you want to, it's about letting the starry night come through. It's about describing, not explaining. When I am writing, I am figuring out where I am. It's almost like psychoanalysis. Sometimes I have an idea of where

I want something to go, but by the time I am finished I realise where I have arrived. Recently I released a song, *Heart of the Matter*. When I reread the lyrics, I realised I had read myself to filth — the song is about how I was scared to love, how I wasn't perfect, how I was broken, how I didn't have the ability to love others as fully as I wanted. That's why I like writing. It can be a painful process but, for me, it is a form of therapy. During the years that I was battling my sexuality, writing would always help me. If I didn't have art when I wasn't talking to God, I think I would have gone crazy. And that means I feel privileged to write.

For the longest time, sexuality didn't feature in my work. When it did come through, it was via identity. If I dip into my back catalogue, I can hear myself asking, 'Who am I?' The breadcrumbs are there. You can definitely hear someone struggling with their sexuality. I think about certain lyrics where I talk about falling again and again. Without facing it head on, that was my opportunity to talk about looking at a guy again for too long. The only place where I explicitly discussed sexuality before I came out was a song called *Broken Images*, where I journaled how I felt I was affected by being addicted to watching porn and how that shaped my behaviour. I don't attribute porn to lust, but as I didn't have any space to pursue my feelings for other guys, porn became a space where I could act out my fantasies. It changed how I saw people. I couldn't walk around without wondering how people looked under their clothes. Art gave me a chance to work that out.

When I came out, I thought about my musical identity. Even though I like to perform in secular spaces, I have good relationships with Christian websites, spaces and conferences. I wondered what those would look like. At the time I remember seeing JGivens, an American Christian rapper, come out. People lost their shit. I wondered how my own coming out would go down with people I knew. While I was performing at a Christian festival, I thought, 'If they knew I'm gay, would I still be here? Would I be welcome here?' I can't hide being black, but I could hide being gay. You know the score. When I was younger, however, I could almost opt out of being discriminated against by not being out. Stepping into my identity as a gay man, I felt that prejudice. At one point, I had an experience that would reflect my feelings at that festival. As part of my old job, I used to lead youth retreats. I had gone to them since I was a child, growing from a young person into a leader and a staff member. Having come out, however, I was told that I might have to stop attending. I hadn't even considered it. The days following were the worst week I have had since coming out. I was brought to a dark place, feeling low and rejected. Eventually I left the job to work at another organisation. It was time to go anyway, but that experience sped up the process. I'm lucky, I know I am accepted in certain spaces, but I still question how I will be accepted more widely. Moving forward, I know that I have to walk away from places that don't accept me.

In 2018, I released *No Man's Land*. It's a very important song to me. I wasn't trying to wave a flag for anyone — gay, or Christian, or both. I was just trying to figure things out. I wanted to work out where I stood. Yet I knew that my music had always been personal. Before coming out I released an EP called *Between Haircuts*, talking about life and honestly asking myself how I was doing. I knew that I couldn't release an EP like that and then hide my sexuality. I took my time with *No Man's Land*, let the process take charge. I wrote parts every two or three weeks, whenever I had ideas, then stitched it all together. I didn't want it to be preachy or come with an end goal in mind. I wanted to create a space where conversations could be had and where people could empathise with the plight of gay Christians. I want people to know how it felt when they asked me questions. I wanted the song to be something that I could have used as a teenager. Not to tell them they have to to come out now, but to make them realise they are not alone and that they have options. I knew the only thing I could do was be personal and honest, to speak from my perspective. It is by far my most revealing song and might be forever — I ain't trying to tell people more of my business!

After I released the song, I had a lot of people message me to thank me, to tell me how the lyrics had helped. Even friends who had been on the journey with me were taken aback and retold me they were there for me. The title *No Man's Land* expresses how I felt: thoughts of suicide, thoughts of walking away from God, thoughts of being lost. I can't speak for everyone, but a lot of gay Christians feel they can't be happy with God as they have to strip their sexuality away, but they can't be happy just acting out their sexuality as God isn't in that. It feels like there is no happy place. Of course, I got some bad responses too. A website that used to feature my music emailed me to tell me they couldn't put the song up as they couldn't be seen to support someone who is openly gay. They took all my music down. One moment they thought I was talking from a faithful angle, the next they thought it all counted for nothing. Ultimately, I am glad I released it. Now people know I'm gay. They can choose whether to accept that or not, and I might have helped some people along the way. I don't know if I will ever make another track as selectively focused on sexuality and faith again. I'm not trying to force a narrative, but I can see it leaking into other parts of my work. Growing up Christian, I was wary about making a track that just screamed, 'Jesus, Jesus, Jesus.' Now I feel the same way about being gay. I'm wary of reducing my art.

There are loads of great queer rappers — Mykki Blanco, Cakes Da Killer, Zebra Katz — but they often get reduced to their sexuality. Like them, I just want to be a dope rapper. My mission is to speak life into people and help them question their worldview. I am a gay, Christian, black, British guy but it's not my job to explain to anyone what being a gay, Christian, black, British guy means. Whenever someone asks me, I have to wonder whether they are genuinely interested or trying to settle a debate. It sucks that you have to have those conversations, but you have to know where you stand. I don't want to write things for the sake of it, but to add to the art. Being in the closet, I self-edited a lot. Now, I want to be honest.

Always thought there's only 2 paths that I could take
Embrace my sexuality or my faith
But what if there's a third?
What if God occurs where there's love and that doesn't just mean him and her?
What if there's a chance that I misread his word?
What if I'm not broke, this is how I'm meant to work?
I don't have the answers but they'll stay unlearnt
Till I leave this no man's land and search

The Worm in the Hand

Siddhi Joshi

Growing up, I was raised in the Hindu faith and lived in India from the ages of two to eight. I have lots of fond memories of India. I come from a big family, many aunts and uncles, and so I had a bustling childhood with so many different things happening. I really connected with my Hindu faith living in Gujarat, and my grandfather was a devout believer of the Hindu God Ganesha (hence my and my sister's names!). We celebrate lots of festivals such as Diwali and Holi. There were lots of temples and the relationship with other faiths was so much more tolerant than in the UK at the moment. In Gujarat, there would be Muslim people living alongside Hindu people living alongside Christian people, Zoroastrians, Sikhs and getting along perfectly well as neighbours. It was very pluralistic at the time — more so than nowadays. It was in primary school that I first felt same sex attraction. Little did I know that Section 377 of the penal code, was still in place. It was only repealed in 2018, essentially scrapped after many campaigns to try and undo the outdated colonial law.

At the age of eight, I moved back to the UK, meaning I have experienced life as an immigrant, regardless of being born in Liverpool. I found it quite difficult to leave my friends and family behind in India. We came from quite a tolerant Hindu middle-class society. We had a very close neighbourhood in India and moving to South London, it was quite a shock because in 1993 there weren't many South Asian families living in the area or on our street. Although most people were very welcoming, we did experience a little bit of racism. I remember when we were growing up there was a time when my brother, my sister and I were playing in the street and there was something in my brother's hand. An old lady came along and kept asking, 'What's in your brother's hand?' because they were sceptical of us playing in the street. When my brother opened his hand, there was just a worm inside. After that, she went away. My brother was saving the worm from being stamped on the pavement, rather than anything more suspicious! Such microaggressions happening from time to time surprised us greatly! The main thing, however, was that life in the UK was a lot more lonely than in India where there were so many more people around and visiting. Sometimes it was very difficult, though we managed to settle in okay — especially as I entered high school. I went to a Catholic school as a Hindu and to gain admission we had to have a certificate from the priest and so my dad had to go to the temple to certify that we were a religious family. It seemed very artificial, but largely I had a positive experience in school. I didn't wish I went elsewhere, I was quite happy at first. I used to enjoy the Religious Education lessons, particularly about marriage, but found the teaching on same-sex relationships discouraging.

In my teens, I began to identify as a lesbian and really discovered my sexuality. I learnt to accept myself and came to terms with my identity. It wasn't always an easy process in the 1990s and the early 2000s. At times it was quite difficult. I found it hard to talk to my parents about my sexuality and to come out to them. And although I kind of came out when I was seventeen or eighteen, it wasn't until my late twenties that my parents and I fully discussed my sexuality, letting them accept it. This meant that I went through quite a rebellious phase. Nothing unusual. During my A-levels, everyone was going through it. I decided to get dreads, which I found a liberating experience (not that I'm associating hair style with any particular values). I would also rebel against my teachers a little bit. My grades began to slip. I felt really rejected by my teachers, like I wasn't being given an equal chance to learn and do my work. They were always asking my parents to come into school.

I don't regret my rebellion that much because I was experimenting with the routes I could take at the same time. I thought that Marine Science would allow me to connect with the natural world and so decided to take it forward at university. University helped me. It solved the problems of teenage years. I went to Southampton to study at the Oceanography Centre. It's one of the leading places to learn Marine Science and I felt that I was finally given a fair chance. Nonetheless, there were a lot of conservative attitudes. Although there was more equality with regards to my education, there were not a lot of Indian people doing Marine Science. There are now, but back then in the early 2000s there weren't. I undertook a placement in Canada for my undergraduate project that went really well, but coming back to Southampton I had problems with my supervisor. He would always think the worst of me. Now, I think it was more homophobia than racism but it's difficult to tell. It was a combination of the two. That was probably the most difficult experience because it was so personal. It was directed at my personality and targeted my character. I didn't feel I could do anything about it at the time. It is hard to hold academics accountable. I felt isolated. I really had to look to my faith for a reason to carry on. I remember reading the Gita for support, learning about my faith that way. Because I had moved to Southampton, it was like I had to find my identity again on my own so when I was having academic problems I found faith was really important. In particular, the stories of Krishna helped to rediscover my spirituality.

At the time that I was discovering Hinduism as an undergraduate, my brother was deciding to become a Buddhist monk. I found it quite difficult. The Buddhism was easy to accept, but the idea of him becoming a monk and not living at home or with my parents was hard. He wasn't even allowed to own money! After I finished my first degree, however, I moved to Galway to continue my education and pursue a PhD. Here, I connected with an undergraduate student I was teaching who also decided to become a Buddhist monk. Now I knew two Buddhist monks, so it pushed me to learn to accept things. I began to see positive changes in my brother since becoming a monk. An elder nun at the monastery said that his love for his family is so deep. This was something which I have always known, but had forgotten because of my anger at the time. I went to the meditation group and learnt about Buddhism. It was really helpful in learning to relate. And it even helped me with my PhD, giving me a sense of mindfulness. When I had work-related stress, I could turn to meditation.

Shortly afterwards, on a visit to India, my auntie and I had the opportunity to visit Ajmer Dargah — the tomb of a Sufi saint, Hazrat Moinuddin Chishti. This is a rare pilgrimage site not only for Muslims, but also Hindus and Christians and Jains, who follow his dream of interfaith harmony in India and the world. I was moved by the relevance of this principle in today's age. Journeys of pilgrimage have helped me to deepen my faith throughout my life and I strive to learn from these experiences and apply them in my day-to-day life. All of this experience led me to set up the British Asian LGBTI group. I thought I needed to do something to help others who might be in the situation I was in. I wanted people who were struggling with their identity to have people that they could turn to. I couldn't tell my family about my sexuality properly at the time, so I thought setting up a network was a simple, easy thing to do. I set up the group on Facebook about six years ago and it's been helping to connect people to each other and to various services, as well as to gain representation. Personally, I had communicated with

Khakan Qureshi (who is included in this book) online. He would always comment on the Facebook page looking to find voices in the community with useful suggestions so I asked him to become an administrator in the group to help improve the network. It was then that we decided to do the South Asian LGBTI Rights conference. It was a wonderful time. Held at the Queen Elizabeth Hospital in Birmingham, we had lots of speakers such as Prince Manvendra Singh Gohil (the first openly gay prince in India), Matt from the Naz and Matt foundation, and Reshma Johar who had a Hindu lesbian wedding. All in all we had eighteen speakers and great intercultural dialogue.

The conference meant everything. It was very powerful. It was like a dream come true, meeting everyone who had been following the group and defending LGBTI rights in person. We created a safe space where people could come forward and voice their concerns and just be accepted for who they are. In South Asian culture there is so much deep-rooted homophobia and prejudice, honour-related violence and the like. Though sexual diversity has been celebrated in Hinduism, in India the colonial laws enacted by the British lasted from 1861 to 2018. These laws all descend from the Buggery Act that has been a huge source of homophobia. Research has shown that ancient scripture is a lot more accepting than the colonial era, which enforced Victorian morality on large parts of India and the British Empire more widely. You find that the laws are still present in some countries. In Singapore they have the same Section 377 that India repealed. These colonial views have become widely entrenched in modern-day mainstream Hindu society — in a similar way to gender inequality. At the conference, we wanted to open a space where people could network and just be accepting of each other.

In Hinduism there are three main gods: Brahma the creator, Vishnu the sustainer and Mahesha the destroyer. All the gods are reincarnations. Krishna is a reincarnation of Vishnu. Shiva is a reincarnation of Mahesha. I really connect with a Shiva deity who has both a masculine and feminine form, Ardhanarishvara. Shiva is a very important god because he is responsible for the circle of life, and destruction is part of that circle. It's about rebirth. You can't always control what is happening with your life, but if you believe in karma then you can be helped in your next life, or even in this one. All the good that you are doing doesn't have to have a reason. Hindus believe that good is carried forward, even when your body is destroyed. Karma means that it is important to have responsibility for your reactions. It's not like sin.Karma is important to me because I want to live by my standards. I hope that my activism is good karma. It has already helped me in the present life. It has helped me to come to terms with my experience of discrimination and isolation. It has made me make something constructive out of the negatives of my life. I'm really happy that I can carry on with the activism because it has helped me so much personally. Currently, I am studying part time for an LLM and volunteering with Amnesty so that I continue to help defend the rights of others. I'm especially interested in fighting human rights abuses.

Faith is really linked to my sexuality, in that I found being in love quite a holy experience. I feel that people who believe LGBTI people cannot have faith are wrong, because I found it a very spiritual experience to be LGBTI and discover my sexual and spiritual identity. In particular, being in love with a woman felt very holy. We had qualities that could complement and improve each other. At school, we learnt about Romanticism and the poems of John Keats. I found that I could really relate to lines like the 'holiness of the Heart's affection' and 'the truth of Imagination'. Similarly, in Hinduism we say that if your heart is pure then what you express will be pure. If you feel hate inside then you are going to express anger. It's really important to be at peace with yourself in order to make a good contribution. This means love is very spiritual.

To me, Hinduism means tolerance. It's about your own relationship with the world around you. It's a spiritual faith, rather than about a particular kind of worship. It's about discovering faith for yourself. There are some aspects, such as the caste system, which I don't agree with. I think to that end, Hinduism has been misinterpreted over the years, but I think when people discover the faith for themselves, they can have a holy experience. Hinduism is about love. Hinduism is about acceptance. Hinduism is about celebrating diversity, about being tolerant of other faiths and orientations, rather than about strict rules. It's why it's so important that LGBTI people are accepted. There are many stories in Hinduism which indicate that you can have more than one or two genders throughout your life. You can have masculine characteristics or feminine characteristics, and so on. There's nothing in Hinduism that says you cannot be LGBTI. Hinduism accepts that you are a lesbian, that there are gay people, that there are transgender people. I think that kind of representation is important. It's only the right-wing conservative mindset that wants to use religion for political purposes and not accept it.

Recently, I came out to my parents properly. Activism helped me to communicate my identity. I thought that they would understand my sexuality, even though I never said, 'I am a lesbian.' The first meeting we had was quite difficult because they weren't expecting it but afterwards they were quite understanding. Now, they are supportive of my activism. Though I don't have a partner at the moment, all they hope is that when I do they are a good person, rather than a particular gender. If I wanted to get married to someone, they would accept it (though I haven't tried that in practice yet!). Family is at the centre of Indian and Hindu culture. I would encourage people to come out to their family if they think that they would be safe. Be honest about how you feel if you can, rather than hide your sexuality.

Everything In Context

Khakan Qureshi

Religion has always been offered to me in layers. When I was younger, I was very religious-minded. I am the youngest of seven siblings and when I was growing up my father was one of the founders of Birmingham Central Mosque, so we were brought up on the nuances of the religion. We could not do things that were haram, we had to eat halal and we had to respect our elders. Though my brothers were Westernised in their outlook — they went clubbing, had girlfriends, and had a lot of male friends — I felt on the periphery of that. I used the Quran as a moral compass, trying to observe what life had to offer and be a compassionate individual. My mother, however, was more liberal and so in my teens I began to become vocal and started questioning the faith. I took the opportunity to read the Quran and question its teachings, inquiring about all sorts of topics. I became fascinated with the similarities between Islam, Christianity and Judaism. I wanted to find out more.

At the same time, sexuality was also offered to me in layers. I grew up in the 1970s and 1980s and there were restrictions at home, at school and in the media. My family lived according to the faith, and being gay was wrong. If a gay couple appeared on television, we had to change channels or leave the room. Concurrently, the press was focused on the HIV and AIDS crisis, the 'gay disease' as it was called, a label that meant the community was treated with stigma and prejudice. Things were no better at school. I grappled with Section 28, which prohibited the promotion of homosexuality in education. I was often bullied, called a nancy and so on. As with my religion, however, I began to question things. I tried not to retaliate but to turn the other cheek and use my voice to question those around me. When I was called a sissy, I would ask what it said about harassment in the Quran or the Bible, to question how someone could call themself a Muslim or a Christian and bully another person.

My drama and music tutors provided the first opportunity for me to interact with people who were proud that they were gay. I admired them for being themselves, for being flamboyant and authentic (though they had to be careful because of Section 28). Nonetheless, I was appalled in some ways. I wondered how people had sex; I kept thinking about the act. I couldn't relate to it as at the time I was more asexual than homosexual. I suppressed my feelings and emotions. At the back of my mind, I was continually thinking about what Allah, what my parents and family would say. Today, we would probably call it internalised homophobia.

After school, I was in a dark place because I didn't get the results that I needed to undertake the degree that I wanted. My drama tutor called me and told me that I had the opportunity to audition for acting college in London. I won a place. Once there, I immersed myself in the culture, but quickly had to take a sharp intake of breath. The other students openly identified as LGBT and I wondered what I had got myself into. When people spoke about sleeping with each other, I was considering my faith and how they were indulging in debauchery. I felt I was much better because I was chaste and saving myself until the wedding night. Though I thought that this made me quite mature, I didn't even recognise the signs when someone was flirting with me. I thought it was just friendly banter! The first time I was actually kissed, I was at a wedding — a marriage of convenience. She was a lesbian, he was gay. I didn't realise that until he tried to kiss me. He was offering me lots of compliments and the next thing I knew, he had kissed me. I was shocked. I didn't want that kind of attention, but at the same time it was my first kiss.

Eventually, I became quite withdrawn, isolated and depressed. I would talk to my housemates about relationships and friendships, about our dreams and ideal partners, but I kept thinking of how my parents wanted me to get married and have children. I wanted to fit into the role model of being a good Muslim boy. Whatever my parents wanted, I was there to make it happen. After a while I met an older student at the college and we bonded. She told me that I wasn't experiencing life, that I wasn't finding out what it was all about. She encouraged me to go out to a bar and see how I got on. I took her advice and I went out to a little place in Charing Cross called Brief Encounter. It took me a long while to pick up the confidence to go inside. When I did several weeks later, I was the only brown face in a white space — and this was 1989. Each time I went in, I kept thinking, 'This is haram, this is forbidden,' and considering the two angels we are meant to have on our shoulders; one angel writes all the good deeds we have done, the other all the bad. I wondered if my bad deeds list would be longer than the good deeds, even though all I was doing was accessing a venue.

One evening, however, I did meet somebody, and had a one-night stand. I was quite excited by the experience and so I kept accessing the venue again and again, but quickly began thinking about the afterlife, as well as worrying about HIV and being nervous that someone might have seen me. I think in that time period, I had about thirteen one night stands, but I believed that I needed to put a stop to it if I wanted to reach heaven. I entered a dark place and contemplated suicide. I was so scared. If Allah wanted me this way, why was I being tested as well? I felt lost. I wanted to end it all. I took myself out of school one evening and headed to a park. I considered throwing myself into the lake. Fortunately, a police car patrolling the park raised its siren and I began thinking about my mum and how she would react if her son took his own life. That made me realise I needed to speak to somebody.

London was not a nice place to be. At college, there were only three Asian people on my course, including myself. The other two were straight and from London, so they had their own networks to rely on. I couldn't make a go of it in the capital, so I returned to Birmingham. People would ask how I was getting on, telling me that my student years were meant to be the best of my life, but I couldn't stop thinking about the one night stands. My niece asked me if I had met anybody and I told her I had experimented, kissed some girls and some boys. I thought it was a fleeting conversation but little did I realise that she had mentioned it to her mum, my sister. I let it go, though, and tried to get on with my life. I wanted to assert my freedom, so I connected with my old friends and started going out. One evening, we went to the local nightclub, which was straight. I got on the dance floor and somebody said 'You don't come out very often do you? You dance like a woman'. So again, I had to box myself in and tried to conform, to do the straight man's dance.

At the same time, I was trying to hit the spotlight as an Asian actor. At one audition, I met another Muslim guy and he told me about somebody who didn't live too far from me, asking if I would like to get to know him. I got talking with the guy who didn't live too far away. There was chemistry. And because there was only a five minute walk between our homes, we would meet up every evening. I didn't realise how strong my connection to him was becoming. I couldn't fight it off, we were just connecting. It took me a while, but after about six months, I initiated the first move. He told me I had been very hard work but that he had liked me from day one, and asked what had taken me so long. I explained that because of my faith, my religion, and my family, I couldn't initially commit myself. My parents were expecting me to get married and have children. He understood. He told me that he wanted me to do whatever makes me happy and that he would follow, even if it meant ending the relationship. That placed me in a position that made me question what I really wanted. I struggled with the cycle of religious doubt again, but this time turned to the Quran to figure out what it said. It was mind-blowing. The world focuses so much on one story — the story of Lut — and they seem to disregard everything else. Every single parable has to be placed into context. You have to look beyond the issues in the book. I realised I ticked all the boxes: I strived to help others, I tried to understand people, I loved nature and children, I was charitable in my own way. I knew that if I took that with me, it would bring me hope. I realised that what I wanted was someone that I could love: companionship, loyalty, someone that would be there for me. I could not fulfill my parents' wishes, it was about me.

Things came to a head one evening when my mum sat me down and asked me what was going on. I told her I had met somebody. Then came the questions: 'Who is she? How old is she? Is she Muslim?' And I had to say, 'No: He's years older, he's white, he's Church of England, he's a skinhead, he has tattoos, he smokes.' Though it was a traumatic conversation, my mum's words will always help me to look forward: 'Whatever makes you happy makes me happy and if I can't share in that happiness, what kind of mum would I be?' It was a different story with my siblings. This conversation triggered a chain of events. My brothers and sisters took me to one side and tried to begin invasive chats with me. I had never queried what they were doing with their lives, but suddenly they were interested in mine. They told me that they were concerned about my wellbeing. I felt like I was being treated like a child. They wanted me to be a good Muslim, but weren't looking at their own behaviour.

I became the elephant in the room. My mum knew, my siblings knew, but my father did not know. Things changed when he found out. My father was a community leader and inclined to think not just about himself, but about his status, his reputation and his relationships with those around him. My parents argued a lot during that time. They talked a lot about religion, asking what the Quran said about being gay, but I had to question them, to add some context. I don't know where I found the strength from, but I did. I told my parents that they had always fought any way and that they had just created another issue out of me.

I withdrew. I took myself away from the family home and became closer to my partner. He was my rock, letting me think it through and consider what I wanted. I realised that I needed to be with him.

Being away from home was heartbreaking for me as I had a close relationship with my mum. I was missing her a great deal. We would have conversations on the phone, but they would quickly become tearful and emotional. One evening my dad told me that I had to come home and speak to them. I was expecting the worst. I wondered if I would have to end my relationship or if I would be packed off to Pakistan. But no. My father opened the door and embraced me. He told me that he could no longer face his lifetime partner being heartbroken. He told me that not having me at home was like losing an arm. He told me that he wanted the family to be complete, for his youngest to come back into the family fold. He spoke about his reputation and what it meant to have a gay son, how he realised it didn't matter, how he loved me all the same. That my dad, who was so anti-gay, could be so accepting, was very strange. For me, that was unconditional love. My parents demonstrated what it meant to be a good Muslim person. They showed what it meant to love an individual. And that's what I take with me.

I have been with my partner now for twenty-six years. The same guy, with the shaved head and the tattoos. Initially my parents met him by default. They wanted to see where I was living and were meant to come over when my partner was out, but they bumped into one another at the doorstep. They got on really well. At that point, my dad began telling me that my household was nice and that my relationship was beautiful. He even brought up the idea of children. It was a shocking but pleasant surprise that my dad, who was in his seventies, offered that to us. And this was a couple of years before adoption was legal for gay couples.

My journey hasn't always been easy, however. At one point I was facing financial difficulties and my brother gave me an ultimatum: I had to set up my own household and go separate ways with my partner to be accepted into the family fold. A few years ago, my mum was in the hospital dying in one ward and my brother-in-law was in another ward. Everyone thought he was dying too. When I went to visit my mum, my siblings told me that I should go and visit him. I was unsure, he had always bullied me, but I did. The first thing he told me was that if I didn't give up my lifestyle and my partner, I would die a death like a dog in the gutter. He told me that Allah would judge me and that if he didn't, he would appear himself on the day of judgement.

Around this time I had begun getting involved with research projects. I had seen younger people struggling with the same issues that I did, and I wanted more than online interaction with other South Asian LGBT people. These experiences drove me to begin working within the community. I do not want to sit here in a number of years and hear South Asian LGBT people say that they cannot come out to their parents. We talk about everything being fine in the mainstream LGBT community but clearly everything isn't fine. In the UK, one of the most democratic countries in the world, people are still living in fear of persecution and oppression at home and in their local communities. We need to break those shackles and change that mindset.

I think we need to have religious leaders on side to tackle the issue. In my role as an LGBT activist, I have asked three imams, 'If an individual comes to you and says that they are LGBT, how would you respond?' Each time they have responded by saying, 'We would offer them advice, information and guidance.' That is good and well, because that is the kind of thing that I would do, but when I ask if they would accept that individual and stand up in front of their community to say it, the response is, 'No, because the community isn't ready.' That is a get-out clause. When is the community going to be ready? I am forty-eight years old now and in my day the community wasn't ready. I don't want anyone having to face negative emotions, to feel isolated and depressed, or to experience trauma like I did. We need the freedom to be who we want to be. We need to remove that level of social inequality.

My dad started his activism in his early forties, the same age I was when I started Finding A Voice, the South Asian LGBT group. Learning about my father over the years, I realised that we clashed so much when I was young because we were so similar. His activism within the community reflects mine. We both want to help others. Growing up I didn't see that. He owned one of the first curry houses in Birmingham. There's a newspaper clipping in the house that says he introduced a thousand dishes to the Birmingham community, not just to integrate the Asian community with the white community, but to integrate South Asians. My parents came to Britain in the 1960s. They saw the signs: 'No blacks, no Asians'. He wanted to push his way through it and develop a level of understanding on both sides. He campaigned in Downing Street, wrote to Buckingham Palace and the BBC. He helped introduce the first language unit to Birmingham. He pioneered a lot of things. He worked for the betterment of other individuals. I feel I am duplicating his work now. I think my dad would be quite proud of me. Like him, I have been to Downing Street, I have been nominated for awards, I write poetry. Whereas my father's activism tried to get people to accept South Asians, I am trying to show you can be South Asian and LGBT. I think he is looking down on me now and I think he would probably laugh, seeing that we clashed for so many years but that we were so similar, both striving to push integration a little bit further.

In the last few years, I have reclaimed the Muslim label. I adhere to the principles of Islam, rather than the five pillars. That's what is most important to me, using the scriptures as a moral compass. A few years ago, I had a conversation with a straight Muslim woman who had studied the Quran. She told me that I was 'more Muslim than Muslim'. When I asked her why, she told me that I gave a completely different perspective. I believe you need to look beyond the literal words in the book, you need to put it into context and use it as a guide to navigate your life.

What I have learnt about faith is that it is about helping the individuals around you. My mum used to say, 'If your heart is good and your heart is pure, then that is all that matters.' My mum went to the university of life and her perception was so insightful. She gave a lot of love. Her outlook simplifies and epitomises what it means to be a Muslim: she fed us, sheltered us, listened to us and accepted us, she took on everyone's baggage and was a pillar of strength. Likewise, who would have thought that my father would have been so proud of me for being gay? For me, that's what it is to be of faith. It is about accepting people regardless of how they identify, about being there for them no matter what they are going through or where they are coming from. In simple terms, religion and scripture are like a set of policies and procedures at work that everyone uses in their own way. The messenger might be different but the message is the same. Whether it is Christianity, Judaism or Islam, it is about helping each other, accepting each other and empowering each other.

Daljinder Johal

My Faith is My Nani

Daljinder Johal

Faith always reminds me of my Nani. I have only really known one grandparent. Both of my dad's parents died when he was very young. On my mum's side, my Nani was quite unique. She was a single mother, divorced when my mum was a child, so it's always been her that we have spent time with. In the school holidays, we would live with her for the entire summer. She doesn't drive and goes to the temple every single day so — unless my uncle and aunt would look after us — we would go with her every morning. This all dictated my early experiences with faith, especially because my Nani was such a big name at the gurdwara. At one point she even had the keys, so was in charge of the running of the temple! We didn't have an elite status because the gurdwara is very much about equality, but it was quite significant to be her granddaughters and, as the eldest, I felt like her representative. For me, faith was always associated with her and therefore was quite comforting. Of course, sometimes it can be quite intimidating to have a huge group of ladies shouting, 'Oh my god, are you Kirpal's granddaughter?' but she would leave my sister and I all day with other people and we knew we would be looked after because there would be so many aunties around (we were always told 'this is your so-and-so's so-and-so's cousin's sister's mother'). We would play with the other kids, be fed and spend the day together. For us religion and faith weren't always about going and sitting and saying Matha Tek or covering our heads. It was being part of a community. It was such a positive thing.

In some ways, I have a hard relationship with my Nani. She's very traditional and expects us to do what she says, but our relationship has always been strong. Because she is so quirky, a lot of my family get annoyed with her, but I don't. As a kid, she worked as a seamstress and would teach us to sew, but she would lie sometimes and say that we couldn't sew after 6pm, telling us it poked pigeons' eyes out. I genuinely believed this! Now, I work in Birmingham a lot and if it's late and the trains aren't running, I'll go to hers. It'll be the dead of night, she'll leave a hot water bottle in the spare bedroom and in the mornings she will make breakfast. I've never even said that I like it (plus it's probably a bit too spicy for me in the morning), but she makes cheese on toast with chutney and because I know she loves making it, I'll sit and eat. Nani has so many friends and the sound I associate the most with her is the phone ringing; she has more of a social life than I do! Really, she is the guru of her temple, not in the traditional sense of a teacher, but in that she's everyone's agony aunt. So even if I'm in a rush, I'll make sure that I schedule time in the morning with her to eat breakfast and fix her phone (undoubtedly, she will have lost her weather app or shut herself out of Facebook).

Speaking of breakfast, for me faith is tied to food. I know everyone says it, but my Nani is the best cook. The woman feeds us! Recently, I was at my cousin's birthday and (though we had already been to Nando's for cake) she wouldn't let us leave until we had eaten more. One big connection between me and my Nani is saag. As a kid, she would tell me and my sister to eat it to become strong like Popeye. Due to all of this, food is love. Cooking is an act of love. At Sikh weddings, we feed each other cake and call it pyaar, which literally means love. Even the time cooking takes is important. Sometimes my friends ask me why I don't cook Indian food more and my response is, 'You don't know how long it takes!' Cooking is also the way that the women in my family connected. It's kind of a patriarchal thing, the men would sit and have a beer and the women would cook, but we had the best time. We would be in the kitchen together, my mum washing, my aunt chopping, me helping — all laughing and joking together. Even as a little girl I can remember sitting on the counter stirring. Me and my sister would fight over stirring, because there's something so soothing and calming about it. Food isn't just a familial love, however. Cooking is also an act of care. As a freelancer, coming home in the evening and cooking for myself is important self-care. I think there's something very primal and instinctual about making food with your hands for another. At the gurdwara, we have langar, a communal shared meal that we make every day. When I was little, my mum told me that anyone could have it. The temple my Nani went to used to welcome a homeless man. He wasn't Indian, he wasn't Sikh, he wasn't Punjabi, but he was never refused. As a child, food was about being nourished physically, mentally and emotionally. It's amazing how intrinsic food is to my faith.

As I grew older, things didn't change with my faith, but it became less a part of my life. Until I was four, I went to a very multicultural school in the middle of a very South Asian area but then I transferred to a very white school on an industrial estate where my sister and I were the only Asian kids. I spoke Punjabi fluently as a child but to look after my interests my parents stopped speaking it to me. They are born here and speak English fluently but they would speak Punjabi to each other when we were little and that completely stopped. On top of this, our parents raised us by themselves. My dad's parents had passed away and my mum's family lived in Wolverhampton so — outside of the summer period with Nani — as we grew older there was less time to go to the gurdwara. Even in comparison to other religions, faith and culture are so intrinsically tied together in Sikhism. There are Sikhs who aren't Punjabi but naturally people associate the two. People don't even realise you can get white Sikhs or Sikhs from other backgrounds. Due to this, pushing down my culture was hard.

Now, I can look back and understand how I pushed away Sikhism in childhood. Even my name marked me out: Daljinder. Most people can't say it. At school, we weren't even really allowed to wear religious clothing like the kara, a steel bangle that you wear on your wrist as a symbol of the Sikh faith. I had to take it off for PE. I went to a very white school and explaining the kara to them as a small child was difficult. I didn't know why I had to wear it because I didn't have the words to articulate it yet. I just knew it was important to me because it was a symbol of my faith. I didn't have a vocabulary, but it was so tied to how I felt about my family. I remember being in Year 5 and there being an India Day. As the only Indian kid in the school, I was looked to. I brought in a bhangra album and I remember my mum had wound it back to my favourite track. The song was Aaja Soniya (Remix) by Bally Jagpal and all the kids laughed at me when it played because it had a recording of a girl at the beginning asking for a remix of the original. The entire class started laughing and I couldn't listen to the song for years afterwards. Because my faith and my culture marked me out as different, they were removed from my life for the longest time. Even when I was bit older (from the ages of nine to fifteen) and we had a few family weddings, I kept those very separate. When I came back with mehndi, I would hide it because the kids would ask why I had shit on my hands. They were quite mean.

In comparison, now that I'm older I am open about weddings, I chat about them and put them on my Instagram. I know for some people that's not a big thing, but for me it is — especially the religious elements. I started to re-engage with my faith positively when I began doing my GCSEs at college. It was more of a mix. Essentially, there was the white high school that I went to and another, brown, high school. Once we started filtering together at college, I was re-exposed. At first, I found it difficult. Now I didn't fit in with white people, but I didn't fit in with the Asians either because I had ignored my culture so much. Where I had engaged with my culture was through cooking and cleaning, which are associated with the traditional Indian girl. I get praise for it now as people say that not many Asian girls know how to cook and clean, but my mum was at college when we were growing up, so it was a survival technique. College allowed me to start engaging with people of other faiths and it was my Hindu best friend who pushed me to positively experience my faith. I envied that she went to the mandir and community events. It reminded me of being a kid again, of spending time with my Nani and all the warmness attached to it.

Though I was beginning to engage with my faith, my sexuality was still an issue. As a kid, I also knew about my sexuality from a really young age. I wasn't exposed to LGBT culture at home, but I remember watching 'All The Things She Said', the t.A.T.u. music video with the women kissing and being like, 'You can do that?!' In Asian culture, however, you don't talk about sexuality — especially for girls, you get married and have a baby and it switches off. It's interesting because I would even have to explain some things to my mum. It's not like Asian kids don't experiment, of course we do, but we just hide it better so our parents don't kill us for it. I went to a very white school and the white kids were more open, so I would come home and tell my mum about the things they got up to (now, I even think she feels quite pleased, because my aunts and uncles have younger kids and she can tell them the things she learnt from me!) Nonetheless, I do think I would have spoken to my mum about my own sexuality more if it wasn't always the big secret. Really, the only exposure I was getting to sexuality were kids saying to each other, 'Oh you're not a lesbian are you? You're not gay are you?' At high school, there were two kids who were Asian and very obviously gay. One of them got away with it because he was so tall that the other pupils wouldn't fight him, but the other one was more petite and I watched the shit get kicked out of him every single day. I remember another time, I was telling a friend that I loved the musician Imogen Heap and she replied, 'Are you a lesbian or something?' It wasn't a big drama but I couldn't even consider it. Ten years down the line, I still remember the sheer panic. Looking back, I wonder if I was such a quiet and closed-off kid because of that, because my sexuality was a secret. I never even admitted the words to myself.

University was the time when I really started to engage with my faith outside of seeing it from afar or through the lens of my best friend. I actually began reading about it and talking to people of the same background rather than ignoring it. It wasn't always easy, people would often ask me to speak Punjabi and I would have to say that I wasn't a performing monkey. This isn't for your entertainment, this is my heritage. University was also the time that I began to explore my sexuality and when I finally admitted it. Up until university, I had avoided all dating as a form of self-protection, but I decided that if I was going to date I was going to do it properly. I was seeing more gay people in the media too, not necessarily Asians, but people I could connect with. I began to feel comfortable and came out to the girl who lived opposite me. She felt safe. She was always talking about sexuality, but I also knew that if she rejected me it was no skin off my nose (although thinking about it now, I probably would have been very highly traumatised!). Her positive reaction led me to think that I had to tell my mum and she was the first person I told after my flatmate. My sexuality had been such a weight so I knew I had to do it. I went home, we were watching TV and I was stressed out of my mind. I just blurted out, 'I have to tell you something,' and my mum began to worry because I was crying. I was barely understandable through tears but eventually I said 'I'm bisexual'. We had a whole conversation and my mum told me it was okay if I was a lesbian. In some ways, it wasn't quite the reaction I was looking for, however. Although my mum was kind about it, she said that my sexuality was always going to be difficult, that even finding someone was never going to be easy. We spoke for hours about what we would tell people.

I came out to my dad the summer after I told my mum. What people don't quite understand is that it's not always that your parents don't love you, but that they do things that upset you without meaning to. My dad would use the word binga, which means bent, to refer to gay people, because there isn't another common word in the Punjabi that they speak (which is probably very different to mainstream Punjabi now, because it's what their parents spoke and taught them). One time, my mum went off at my dad about it, telling him to just use the word 'gay' instead. In the end, I came out during an argument with my dad about something completely different because my mum screamed 'You've gotta tell him!' He stopped the argument and gave me the positive reaction that I needed. We cried a bit, he hugged me and told me it didn't matter. It's strange however, because it made me realise where my mum was coming from. Unlike my mum, my dad is the type to ignore realities. He would rather not talk about it. So even though it was the loving reaction I appreciated, I understand why mum worried.

It's always very hard to explain to white people what it meant for me to tell my parents about my sexuality. Even though I knew me and my mum were so close, there was always the fear she could reject me. It's more than that though. In the way Asian families work, it is just us. We are a unit. And so my sexuality wasn't just a weight because of me, but because of the consequences of making my mum's life harder. My job has always been to make my mum's life easier. Not many kids wake up, cook breakfast, clean the kitchen, go to school, come home and make roti for their parents, but my mum studied while I was at college so I had to look after her. When I came out to my dad, my mum was ready to pack her bags and leave if he reacted badly. It's hard to explain to white people how much that means. There's a scene in the film *Bend It Like Beckham*, when the older sisters asks the young one 'Do you always want to be the girl who married the white guy?' I relate to that film so much. It's important to me for so many reasons, both because Asians aren't often seen as attractive (we are just portrayed as terrorists or victims) and because it showed me things that I didn't know were possible.

When I was younger, bi was the first term that seemed to fit. Existing in the straight world, people always think that means you are slutty. There are so many bisexual myths. In the LGBT community, however, white people also often ask why I identify as bi rather than as pan or queer, saying that bi excludes non-binary and trans people. Again, these are terms white people invented. A white woman coming out as bi is very different to a brown woman coming out as bi, even though people try and project the image onto me. It's hard explaining to my parents who have never met someone who isn't straight (especially when it's their own daughter telling them) so I have to pick my battles. Overall, I still like the term bi, but sometimes I don't feel like it fits — that's because of other people though, not because of me. It's the same thing with queer. A white queer person's experience of the world is so different. People will even ask me, 'How can you be South Asian and gay?' They seem like two alien concepts to bring together. I don't think there should be a special term for people of colour, but I find it so hard to respond.

I think I have a hard time with labels anyway. I have a disability, type 1 diabetes. It even takes me a while when I enter spaces for people with disabilities to realise, 'Oh, this is me.' It's not that I forget I have diabetes, it's that I forget it counts under that because it's less visible. I feel very invisible in my identities. Even though diabetes is so visible, I will cover it up by injecting privately, especially at freelance jobs. I shouldn't do it and it isn't intentional, but it makes me feel more comfortable (even if it perpetuates the cycle of me being uncomfortable). Even with my Asian identity — especially as a Sikh Punjabi with quite light skin — I won't tell people what I am. I have lived abroad but even in the UK, if people haven't met Punjabis before they don't register you as being Indian. They just think I'm Mediterranean. I always get 'Where are you from?' People at university who were from London would ask and I would have to say 'We are in Warwick, this is the Midlands, this is my ends'. It's the same with being bi. I won't tell co-workers immediately but I will if it comes up, if we are talking about dating for instance. It's a privilege, of course, because I am quite femme-presenting so I don't get slurs thrown at me as I walk down the street, but at the same time it's quite hard because I haven't always been in an environment when it's been safe. It's also not the most automatic thing, because I still do have to exist in environments with my Asian family who are more conservative on my dad's side. I can't tell them about the girl that I'm dating, so I end up tending to say nothing.

I think my own sexuality is why I shout so much about representation in my job, which is freelancing across journalism, marketing and production. I would just say I'm arty. I was the kid who read the *Encyclopaedia*, I always wanted books. Plus, I was really nosey and wanted to ask questions. Now, I find that even if I can be quite closed off, I am able to articulate myself in words. I knew that if I was going to make a difference in this world, I wanted to make one person like me feel less alone. I started off working for my student newspaper at university and realised how much I resonated with some of the shows I was reviewing. I asked why we aren't talking about these issues more and that led me to seek out more opportunities for doing so. Because of this, representation is a small slice of the pie in regards to what I want to do. I want there to be more opportunities for people of colour, for LGBT people, for disabled people, for working-class people and for neurodivergent people in the arts. I want to help build people up to be in more senior positions, to organise networking events, and to have support groups that aren't just a bunch of white women drinking champagne and talking about how hard things have been. This all led me to working for Gaysians. It was a series of happy accidents, but when musician Reeta Loi who runs the group put out a call for a Web and Marketing Manager, I applied and she already knew who I was. It was the weirdest thing. Apparently, my article about bisexual myths had been passed around within their networks. Reeta is so supportive and inspirational, she gives me room to grow without babying me. It's as easy as breathing with her.

Today, I know that Sikhism means my future. Sikhism is what I'm going to do with the rest of my life. Marriage comes into it. I'm an old woman now, my cousins have all got married and everyone has started to ask when I will. Even though my Nani knows that I'm bi now, her preference is still for a Sikh Punjabi man with a dastaar and without cut hair, so I know my relationship with Sikhism will be complicated by the fact that I am bi, especially with Sikhism becoming more fundamental in the UK. Even if I were to marry a guy who wasn't from a Sikh background, I wouldn't be able to get married in the temple, which is what a wedding is to me. Atheists often ask why it matters, but I've seen all my family get married in the temple, that's what a wedding is to me: rituals, food, parties. There's nothing in Sikhism that says homosexuality is bad. Men and women are also meant to be equal. It's the Punjabi patriarchal culture that corrupts the faith and causes inequality. This is why I value Sikhism so much, because there's a parity there. Equality is so fundamental to pure Sikhism. The religion includes so many teachings that are important to me as a person and principles which resonate with my own values. Sikhism is also all about balance. Sikhs are meant to be warriors and fight for what you believe in. I'm not going to be picking up a sword anytime soon (I wouldn't get very far, I'm five-foot-nothing!), but it's why I do the job that I do. It's why I fight for representation. It's why I cause a bit of a ruckus. Sikhism is why I won't just stand down.

Conversation Across a Table

Ben & Robert

I meet Ben and Robert in London at the end of summer. Robert picks me up from the underground station, explaining they have to be out of town later that day as they are caring for Ben's cousin, who was injured during the Second World War. Their stylish flat is filled with photographs, art, and ceramics. Ben offers me coffee as Robert talks about the decriminalisation of homosexuality, recalling a pair of friends who became a couple when it was still a crime to love another man. We sit together at their dining table under a large painting of Saint Teresa of Ávila and an angel. I am at the head, with Ben to my right and Robert to my left, facing one another. As we begin to record, I sweep the Dictaphone between them but before long they have begun to push it towards one another. They seem to know, instinctively, when the other has something to add. A clock chimes at regular intervals. I listen to their story and the angel watches over us.

SR: How did you meet?

Ben: We met through mutual friends on the 3rd of May 1971. They came to see me in my house in my second appointment and we got on well and took it from there.

Robert: I was a student at the time and one of our friends had also been a student at the college I was at. I was looking for Confirmation and the college chaplain was totally useless so the friend said 'I know a priest in London who will help you'. I was introduced to Ben and the rest is history.

Ben: That's absolutely right. Robert was preparing for the sacrament of Confirmation and after that we continued to see one another, except Robert went away for six months to Paris and to work on the Channel ferries during the holidays so it became obvious it was a time of testing of acceptance and we got on with it.

Robert: When I came back from studying in Paris, life went on and developed from there.

Ben: I was living in a clergy house and Robert was living in digs in North London for the first three years of our friendship. It wasn't until I moved to my third job and had a vicarage of my own that we were able to move on from seeing one another without a base.

Robert: To setting up home.

Ben: To setting up home.

Robert: So, we started setting up home three years into our relationship and have lived together ever since.

Ben: That's right.

SR: So you were already a priest at the time?

Ben: Yes, I had been a priest since 1967. When Robert and I met I was responsible for a chaplaincy job looking after young graduates in universities and teachers from colleges of education. I allocated them to groups all over the country, including one in central London in the house where I was working and the church where I was working. It was a specific job and then I moved into general parish work. That's where the vicarage turned up. I became the vicar of a church in London for thirty-two years, then I retired — or we retired!

Robert: Yes, we always were determined, although there is an eight-year age difference between us. We always knew there would be consequences if we retired together as I was a non-stipendiary priest meaning I had a 'proper' job as well (this was an 'in' joke between us!). I was a schoolmaster and would be retiring before my pensionable age but we planned for that, well ahead, and we were very happy to retire together and to have the time we have had. We have had twelve years of retirement and it has been highly productive for us.

Ben: That's right.

SR: Were you raised a Christian?

Ben: I wasn't actually but I went to Cambridge and I realised that something needed to be done about this issue. I got myself Confirmed using the college chaplain and after that things developed. I went to read natural sciences — physics, chemistry, maths, biochemistry — but my sense of the presence of God emerged naturally. I had to act on it and I did. About six months after I had been Confirmed and become a regular communicant, my vocation developed and I changed to read theology. My whole life developed from there and I have not regretted a minute of it.

SR: **What was the feeling that brought you towards faith?**

Ben: A sense of the numinous, a sense of presence, and a sense of my own inadequacy or, to use a more technical word, unworthiness led me to discuss it with the chaplain. It worked out very well. It was a sense of wonder. If I want to look at any one thing that actually developed that, the answer is the hymns we sang at school. There are many great hymns in the Anglican tradition, sadly some of which have been jettisoned. The words are actually extremely good. I loved good words: 'Oh measureless might, ineffable love.' Ineffable. It's a word you roll your tongue around and it makes your mind boggle. I have forgotten how it goes on. 'Oh measureless might, ineffable love…'

Robert: 'While angels delight to hymn Thee above.'

Ben: 'Thy humbler creation though feeble their lays, with true adoration shall' — and this was the word in the hymnbook — 'lisp to thy praise.' The word lisp indicates an impediment. In other words the human condition has an impediment in it if your worship is going to be acceptable. The word lisp has been removed because it's politically incorrect but removing it has knocked out the whole meaning of the verse, effectively. It was hymns like that. Another popular hymn: 'Angels, help us to adore Him ye behold him face to face.' Take out the comma and it doesn't mean very much. Leave the comma in and it becomes an invocation. That sort of language is the language which has led me into a life of contemplative prayer, adoration and service.

SR: **That's really beautiful, thank you. Robert, what brought you to faith?**

Robert: We are very different people. Human beings are intellect and emotion. Ben works from the intellect into emotion and I work from emotion into the intellect. I think children around the age of six or seven become self-aware and, in becoming self-aware, become aware of the 'Other'. Around that age, I spent a lot of time alone. There was much more freedom for children in those days and I was just acutely aware of the presence of God. That is a joy and a strength that has never left. Intellectually I don't think I can explain that. It was just always there. It makes me a poor evangelist because I don't understand the idea that one could not be aware of the presence of God because I have always had it as a gift and I come from a completely non-religious background apart from births, deaths and marriages.

Ben: And grandma.

Robert: And grandma. My grandma. I only knew one of my grandparents. My grandma worshipped at the parish church. At eight o'clock on a Sunday morning she went to Holy Communion and in the afternoon she went to a Baptist chapel along the road to sing hymns and 'praise the Lord'. She lived at these two poles of religious experience but she was always singing hymns and my mother did too, although we didn't go to church. I was surrounded by the singing of hymns. I knew the words to hymns and like Ben I think the words resonated.

Another part of this awareness of the 'Other' is that I was brought up in Dover, so I was always aware, on most reasonable days, of another place that you could see across the sea. The line on the horizon. The one thing that I always wanted to do was to go to that other place. To discover the 'Other'. I think my religious experience and this go together. I started finding French radio and listening. Of course, I didn't understand a word, but I had picked up a lot of words by the time I had started learning French and it was the only thing that I ever wanted to learn. Along with that awareness of the other was an awareness that God was calling me to be a priest. I had nightmares as a child because I did not know how to organise the services and choose the hymns. It was something that woke me constantly as a child.

God and I battled over this for a number of years. I wanted to be a schoolmaster and teach French and God wanted me to be a priest so we agreed a compromise. I was a schoolmaster and a priest for most of my life.

SR: You have both spoken about hymns. Have these been an important part of your relationship?

Ben: The short answer is no. The thing that has been at the heart of our relationship is the Eucharist and our time together, every day, saying morning and evening prayer. Times of silent prayer together and the Eucharist together, is that fair?

Robert: Yes, and we both have a strong sense of the presence of God in our different ways. We can be together in silence, not just in prayer. Having said that, as people who practice contemplative prayer, we are never not in prayer and are very comfortable together in silence. On a long drive, sitting reading in the evening, out on a walk, the silences are productive and tangible.

Ben: That's right.

Robert: We don't have to fill every moment with…

Ben: With chatter.

Robert: We do communicate in silence.

Ben: We often say something and the other has already been thinking about it. That's not unique, it's often true for couples who have been together for many years. They intuitively interact at a level that is below vocal and know what is going on before it is expressed.

Robert: Ben is right about the Eucharist. It's something that we never pass up on. We have a house rule that if possible we don't travel on a Sunday. If we have to travel, then it is in the second half on Sunday. It's not religious legalism, it's because we know that our place is at the Eucharist. It's where we want to be, even if we are not celebrating the Eucharist. If we go abroad, we go to our local church, wherever it is. In France, in Italy, wherever, we will go to mass at the local church in order to be at the Eucharist, to be in the presence of God in that thanksgiving way, and to be together.

Ben: And to be within the community of faith. Christianity is a corporate religion and there is no such thing as a single Christian. We all belong to the body and it is important always to keep in touch with the body and be there as part of the body.

Robert: The Eucharistic body is fundamental to us. Because I was a non-stipendiary priest in Ben's parish, it was the basis of all our mission work in that parish. All our pastoral work in that parish was to build the body, the holy people of God. It was highly successful and very rewarding for us. In central London, an almost unidentifiable community formed around the Eucharist. The Eucharist was the call and we had people from all four corners of the globe and all four corners of the Christian experience. We even had some Anglicans! That's my little joke because we had everything.

Together, laughing: Russian Orthodox, Greek Orthodox, Lutherans, Free Church, Methodists, Presbyterians, lots of Roman Catholics.

Robert: We had every sort of Christian without compromising the Eucharist. Everyone was welcome to our Eucharist, but it was the Eucharist the way the Church of England celebrates it. Always with an open door and an open heart. Everyone was welcome. If they felt able to join us, we were welcoming to them from their tradition.

Ben: We had a motto: 'A Diverse People, Enquiring Minds and Open Hearts'. We didn't play the game of dumbing down. We gave them nourishment for Monday, Tuesday, Wednesday, Thursday, Friday and Saturday so they were back again the following Sunday. We didn't go in for cheap tricks.

Robert: Nor did we set hurdles that people had to jump.

Ben: We accepted that people lived very busy lives in central London. There were no endless societies. It was just worship and hospitality. We entertained every Sunday, perhaps ten or twelve people to dinner, and we mixed and matched the people. As the congregation grew, so that grew as well. It was a very important aspect that they practiced hospitality to one another. They actually supported one another, they got to know one another, they did business together! It became a really cohesive community and grew substantially.

Robert: When Ben became the vicar, it had a congregation of about thirty, largely middle-aged to elderly with a handful of children at the younger end. When we retired there was an electoral roll of five-hundred-and-fifteen, a mailing list of over eight hundred and a regular Sunday attendance of over three hundred. It was year-on-year gentle but continuous growth based on inquiring minds and open hearts. It was an extremely diverse congregation: ethnically, socially...

Ben: Some people were very poor, some were immensely rich. Right across the board. A child befriending another child doesn't take any note of the parents' positions financially, socially or ethnically. They just make a friend. And that put parents in touch with parents and the whole thing coheres.

SR: You're married, aren't you?

Robert: No, we have a Civil Partnership. We're not allowed to marry, not allowed by the church.

SR: What did the Civil Partnership mean to you?

Ben: It meant an extraordinary amount. We saw it in terms of its financial benefits, its emotional benefits, its health benefits — hospital benefits and so on. We entered into a Civil Partnership on the 7th of January...

Robert: 2006.

Ben: 2006, just within a few weeks of the legislation going through. What it actually did for us in the end, on the day, was to bring home that we were recognised by the state as being partners. There was a legal officer acknowledging the reality we had experienced since 1971. That really was it. The registrar said to us, 'Straight people who come to get married just assume they can take it. What we have recognised is that people in your position appreciate it.' I said, 'Give it ten years.' What we appreciated was the change in status.

Robert: It came out of the blue. We hadn't been following the early days of the Bill in Parliament. It just suddenly appeared so we hadn't given it an awful lot of thought until the last moment. It was a surprise.

We had to be very careful. As it had happened so quickly the Church was falling over itself to try to come to terms with this idea. The first Civil Partnerships were on the 19th of December 2005. That explosive day. We were going to be retiring in July 2006 but nobody else knew that. Our parish had Buckingham Palace in it and as the Church was not entirely happy with Civil Partnerships, it could have been a very good headline in the seedier press: 'Queen's Vicar Weds' — you can see the interplay of ideas there. The balloon would have gone up with the Bishop of London and our retirement, instead of being a happy event with our people, could have been a difficult one.

Just as with heterosexual marriage the banns have to go up publicly in City Hall for a number of weeks. Looking at it, because of the Christmas and New Year season, for many days at the end of December City Hall was going to be closed. We thought that after the razzamatazz of Elton John the publicity would be finished and that it would be old hat by the first week of January. So we fixed our Civil Partnership for the 7th. As witnesses, we had an Anglican bishop from another country and a member of the Conservative Party in the House of Lords. Two friends witnessed our new wills, a couple who were heading for their sixtieth anniversary together, very conscious that just for loving each other they had been criminals when they first met. There were just six of us. We kept it very low-key. No one knew it was happening unless they had read the banns.

It was a very moving occasion. The interesting thing was that the generational slip was already happening. In our room there were six of us. In the next room, which was huge, there was a young couple and it was morning wear, a string quartet playing and hundreds of guests. It was a big, public occasion, whereas ours was still very much in secret. Nonetheless, rewarding. We could have had a big room, if we had been prepared to risk the wrath of the Church. The congregation would have turned out in droves. We had always circumvented an antagonistic society as much as possible. We always had wills and declared each other to be next of kin, but it is nice to be able to say, 'My Civil Partner.' Purely on emotional grounds however, I would like to have a Church wedding before we die.

SR: What would that mean for you?

Robert: It would be the final piece in the jigsaw. We are accepted before the state and before the law. It would be good, publicly, to be accepted by the Church and in the eyes of God. We know that we are accepted in the eyes of God, but the Church still says this is not acceptable. It would be simply that final recognition that who we are and what we are was made, loved, and blessed by God. We have been baptised, we have been confirmed, we have been ordained, we have received the Eucharist. These are all the major sacraments...

Ben: We have been penitents, we have been to confession, we have been anointed in times of illness.

Robert: Six out of seven, including all the major sacraments. And still now the Church would not deny us, were we not baptised, baptism. We would be baptised, we would receive absolution as penitents, we would be ordained. Marriage, in a sense, is a lesser sacrament to these but we are denied it. It is that incompleteness, that hole in the puzzle, that I would like to see filled.

Ben: Although people are ordained who are gay, it is on the proviso that they are celibate, which is hypocrisy written large. There is a document that you are supposed to read and assent to but in the end, who is going to witness how you live? A former Bishop of London said that 'I cannot act against gay priests unless I have two witnesses,' which is effectively saying, 'I'm not doing anything about this.' They recognise that quite often gay people have a wider sensitivity, partly because they have been persecuted and therefore their antennae are very sensitive, but also because they use much more of their full character, in terms of the feminine and masculine, than many straight people actually explore. I would say a good priest is someone who has a wide spectrum of sensitivity and many gay priests have it. To lose that would be to lose a whole section of fruitful ministerial experience, which would be very sad.

Robert: I would add that current positions in the Church of England make it look ridiculous. It may not be that people are not going to church or that they lose their faith, but it creates a general atmosphere to the modern metropolitan world. Most people have someone in their family who is gay. Most people know someone who is gay outside of their family. Most people know someone who is gay in their company. Because we have become much more visible, the level of acceptance is higher. There is still hate crime and it is terrible but it is relatively small. The image of the Church is damaged in its negativity, especially when it takes away the potential for the Church to speak out against hate crime. Whilst the Church is not committing gay hate crimes, it is forcing people into hypocritical positions and potentially the negativity is what feeds hate crime.

SR: Following from that, I have to ask a slightly difficult question. Have you faced many difficulties in being together and being priests?

Ben, laughing: It's not a difficult question.
Robert: It is quite an easy question really.
Ben: Bishops know everything. That's the first thing. You know they say one thing and in fact they rely on gay priests to run so many things

that in the end they can't avoid this issue. Of course, they do, publicly, but privately they let you get on and do what you want. Robert was licensed to the parish where I was the incumbent, and the Bishop of London knew perfectly well. He had actually stayed in our house, in our vicarage. He called us his friends, he stayed overnight, he fed from our table. He knew perfectly well what the score was. It isn't easy, it's actually a deceptive way, but we understand why the bishops are stuck.

I have never personally experienced any prejudice from members of my congregation or the hierarchy. It took twenty-two years for someone to ask a direct question about it but were always out together for dinner and all the rest of it. People came round to dinner at the vicarage and we were at the head of the table together, it was obvious. For them it was irrelevant, not an issue.

The only thing to say is that if you have to choose between ambition and happiness, choose happiness because you don't get preferment. The more you are up the ladder the more public your life becomes. When you are a parish priest you have a public life and as far as the laity are concerned, there has never been an issue whatsoever. Set not your heart on the support of princes, because it doesn't work out. I always say, and it's a bit of a cliché, that the cause is greater than the issue. The actual proclamation and living of the Christian faith is far more important than the particular issue. It means that you are available to people of the same gender and orientation as you, and people who are different from you. It's all, in a sense, irrelevant. Robert, I believe, feels our relationship has held me back. That's not how I see it at all. What I see is that my life is a fulfilled and happy one in the context of my faith and my professional life. I never wanted for more because those who go for more end up, by and large, disappointed.

SR: Thank you. To finish, you said that you know that God loves you. What does that mean for you?

Robert: The bottom line is that when all else fails, or appears to, I know, like Job, that my Redeemer liveth. Not in an intellectual sense, I know in the core of my being that God made me as I am. According to the Genesis myth, God looked and saw that the world was very good. I think that's God's experience in ongoing creation: as the creation goes on and on and on, God looks at it and sees that it is very good. I know that God loves me because if he didn't, I wouldn't exist. If God turned away, we wouldn't be here. I believe that God has redeemed me from myself and my faults and that one day I shall stand, in his presence, and worship.

Rabbi Mark Solomon (photo: Ajamu)

Holy Books

Rabbi Mark Solomon

My relationship with religion has been at the centre of my life, all my life. It has often been a troubled relationship, but it is still there. Along with being gay, faith is the main thing that defines who I am. I was born into a Jewish family and had a strong Jewish upbringing right from the beginning. From a very early age, though, I was aware of other religions and fascinated by them. So although I am Jewish and a rabbi, it has never been a completely exclusive relationship — there has always been a strong engagement with other faiths, particularly Christianity and Islam. On an institutional level, I am very engaged with the Jewish community. As well as my two congregations and my position as an interfaith consultant, I am a senior lecturer at Leo Baeck College (where I have been teaching rabbinic students for twenty-six years or so) and the associate chair of the Beit Din (rabbinic court) of Liberal Judaism, so I am part of the authority structure there.

At the moment, I tend to see my religious life falling into three clear periods. During the first period, from childhood until I came out in my twenties, I held quite a traditional view of faith. I believed in the traditional, patriarchal Jewish God who is the giver of the Law and who judges, rewards and punishes you. I wasn't clear about what that reward or punishment looked like — Jews tend not to discuss those details much — but it was the basic outline of my faith. I was brought up in Sydney, Australia, in a religiously traditional family, going to a fairly relaxed modern-Orthodox synagogue. My mother was very involved (my father less so) and the synagogue was at the centre of my life for many years. At about the age of around ten or eleven, I had become friends with the children of the rabbi (who was my hero) and I developed a desire to become really orthodox, much to the horror of my parents, especially my father. I started wearing a kippah at school and secretly walking to the synagogue on Saturday, because you aren't supposed to drive on the Sabbath if you are orthodox. Someone spotted me on the five-mile walk one day and lots of trouble ensued, with faith becoming a running battle between me and my father throughout my teens. By fourteen I knew I wanted to be a rabbi. Shortly afterwards, a rabbi from the Lubavitch community started coming to my state school once a week to give lessons in Tanya, their mystical holy book, during lunch break. Habad-Lubavitch is an ultra-Orthodox Hasidic sect that does a lot of outreach work. I had already been interested in Hasidism from a distance, but now I became completely hooked.

At that time, the only yeshiva (religious seminary for young men) in Australia was in Melbourne. My parents weren't happy about me going, but they still supported me, and I began staying there during my school holidays. The yeshiva became a haven for me. Being frank, one of my problems as a teenager was masturbation. When I had my bar-mitzvah at thirteen, I was given a Code of Jewish law, and of course the first thing I looked up were the bits about sex and the dreadful stuff it had to say about masturbation (it's worse than murder, since you are killing all of your potential children, supposedly!). This really blighted my teenage years as I suffered horrific pangs of guilt, especially believing in a traditional Big Brother view of God who is always watching. The first time I was at the yeshiva, however, I didn't 'sin' the whole time. I thought, 'This place is so holy, this is where I need to be.' So when I finished high school (having become more and more religious), I wanted to go to the yeshiva full time. My parents reluctantly allowed me to put off going to university for a year (which turned into two years) to study in yeshiva. At some point, it had become obvious that my fantasies were gay, but it was the masturbation itself that was the main source of guilt. The yeshiva is an all-male space and I began to develop strong crushes on other boys. You go to the mikveh (ritual bath) every morning and immerse together for spiritual purification, so I would see them naked. I lasted a few weeks without masturbating, but when I did succumb it was a crushing disappointment.

Despite the challenges, the community was wonderfully warm and embracing and I got deeply involved in it. I already wanted to be a rabbi, so I decided to stay for a second year. During this time I began having more and more serious religious problems. These stemmed from the problem of Jewishness and non-Jewishness as it is presented within the Tanya. As a child, I had been brought up with Modern-Orthodox thought which is quite universalistic, so although I believed that Jews had a special God-given task, I did not think that they were better than anyone else. Now I was faced with a mystical text that said otherwise, presenting Jews as fundamentally different, as essentially godlier. I was shocked and, though I tried to accept it, this view ultimately did not fit with me. My closest friends at school were non-Jews, and a lot of our friendship was based on religious discussion. One was a religiously-minded agnostic and the other an Anglican (he later converted to Catholicism and became a friar for several years), but the idea that they were spiritually fundamentally different from me didn't make any sense. One of our favourite activities after school was to go 'church hunting', visiting churches all over Sydney and admiring the architecture. (If the vestries were open, we would go in and admire the vestments — and put them on if no-one was around!) We were obviously quite odd teenagers. Not interested in sport or girls, just getting books out of the library and poring over cathedrals. Not very surprisingly, both of these best friends also turned out to be gay. At the yeshiva, I became more and more dissatisfied with the answers I was being given about the Tanya. I began doing my own research and became seriously rebellious and disruptive. On the surface it was all about this religious problem — what I came to call metaphysical racism — but under the surface was a lot of repressed sexuality and problems with depression. In the end, I was asked to leave, though I had learnt an awful lot.

Still wanting to be a rabbi, I turned back to modern-Orthodox Judaism, and in 1983 I headed to Israel to attend Bar Ilan University near Tel Aviv, where you could undertake rabbinic studies in the morning and a degree in the afternoon. I arrived in Tel Aviv early with vague ideas of joining a kibbutz before university, but I visited some Aussie Lubavitcher friends in Kfar Habad and took the easy, if ultimately unhelpful option of staying in the huge yeshiva there. My questioning and dissatisfaction became even more intense, and in June 1983 I decided I couldn't be Jewish anymore. By then it seemed to me that Judaism itself, not just this particular Hasidic sect, was infected with metaphysical racism, so I decided to be agnostic instead. I managed that for about two weeks, at which point I found myself powerfully drawn towards the idea of converting to Catholicism. This was deeply disturbing. Although my best friend was a Catholic and I had a passion for church architecture and music, for traditional Jews the Roman Catholic Church is the ultimate enemy. I started reading more and more about Christianity, reading the New Testament for the first time, and left Kfar Habad to stay at Bar Ilan.

I only lasted for one semester at university in Israel and decided to go back to Australia, with my first visit to Europe *en route*. On January 4th 1984 — a date engraved on my memory — I stepped onto the plane bound for Rome and took off my kippah, which I had put on the first day at high school. In Italy, France and England I visited as many cathedrals as I could, and saw the Pope consecrating bishops from all over the world, which symbolised for me the universal nature of Christianity. Back in Australia, I studied English (lots of Christian poetry) and History (lots of Church controversies) at university, while pursuing the idea of converting to Catholicism. I was deeply attracted by its universalism and the idea of the Incarnation, that God had become human and shared in our agony. I was leading a strange double life, living at home with my parents, singing in the synagogue choir and teaching at the Sunday school, but also attending mass — often at a rather camp Anglo-Catholic church — and spending university holidays in the Carmelite monastery where my friend was living. Part of what held me back from eventually converting was that I thought it would kill my mother, but part of it was that the conviction never became strong enough; Christianity, just like Judaism, also contained particularism and I wasn't finding the answers I was looking for. In the latter months of 1987, my last year of university, quite out of the blue, I found myself being drawn to the synagogue during the High Holy Days. On Rosh Hashanah, instead of just turning up to sing in the choir, I felt moved to attend the earlier part of the service. A few days later on Shabbat Shuvah (the Sabbath of Return), I was attending the Saturday evening service in a routine way with my parents, when I had the most powerful spiritual experience of my life. Instead of letting my thoughts wander as usual during the silent Amidah (the main prayer) I started to really pray, and then had a very intense moment of awareness, a sort of revelation, in the form of an overwhelming conviction that I could never be anything but Jewish and that I *had to* be a rabbi.

The second period of my religious life was sparked by my coming out, which began in the summer of 1989. The previous autumn I had arrived at Jews' College, the modern-Orthodox seminary in London, and my first year was very happy. During the long hot summer of '89, I was really on my own for the first time ever. I had just turned twenty-six and was aware of the stirring and disturbing sexual feelings inside myself when a film called *Torch Song Trilogy* was released. I saw it at a tiny underground cinema in Piccadilly Circus and was blown away, seeing it twice more in quick succession. In my life up till then Judaism had been the major element. I was aware of homosexual feelings, but they were associated with the momentary aberrations of masturbation. Nothing had brought Judaism and homosexuality together; they were in hermetically sealed compartments. The central character of *Torch*

Song Trilogy, an extremely Jewish New York drag queen, broke that barrier down. It was the catalyst that breached the iron wall that separated faith and sexuality. I could no longer ignore it. I started gingerly exploring gay life, going to a Jewish gay and lesbian group, seeing the few gay-related films that were on, reading about it as much as I could. My relationship with God became one of massive guilt. I would describe praying during that period as spiritual self-flagellation, a painful experience. I had heard of Rabbi Lionel Blue previously from Carmelite friends. He had come out publicly in the summer of 1988 — he was tipped off that the *News of the World* was going to do an exposé so he came out in *The Guardian* to forestall them. I read a book he had written called *A Backdoor to Heaven*, a spiritual autobiography with a gay subtext. It was such a beautiful book that I thought I had to make contact. I'll never forget the first time I went to see him: I walked into his living room in Finchley and, to my astonishment, he said, 'Hello Ducky!' Lionel became a great source of strength, support and friendship. The first thing he did was send me to his therapist, a very difficult process but ultimately rewarding, and also introduced me to his gay friends. Lionel encouraged me to finish my studies and get ordained, so that's what I did.

In 1989, I returned to Australia for my annual visit. I had always had a very difficult relationship with my younger sister who had turned against Judaism in her teenage years. I went down to Canberra, where she was studying, and we began to talk properly for the first time. At that point, I wasn't quite ready to say 'I'm gay', but I told her I was bisexual, and she shared with me some very personal things about her life and feelings. Suddenly, from having no relationship, we became very close. I think she went from seeing me as a weird, holier-than-thou, arrogant prick to seeing me as a human being. A year later I came out to my parents. On that visit to Sydney, a Catholic priest friend who was coming out urged me to see his therapist, where I attended some group sessions with other men, most of whom were gravely ill with AIDS. It became clear I was in an even bigger mess emotionally than they were! At my final session, two days before flying back to London, the therapist asked me directly, 'What do you need to do to move on?' and I said I needed to tell my parents. He asked, 'When will you do that?' and I said, 'Well, I suppose tonight,' so after a couple of stiff whiskies, that's what I did. My mother wept. My father, however, who had a savage temper, and with whom I'd scarcely spoken civilly for years, calmly began asking questions and making notes in a pad. That night, I went to meet friends at a gay bar and got picked up by a guy for the first time. It seemed very symbolic. The following day, my mother told me my father wanted to talk to me and we had the first adult conversation of my life, in which he shared with me challenges he'd faced and overcome. Just talking with my father calmly and kindly was an amazing experience. As soon as I got back to London, I ventured out to my very first drag show at the Black Cap in Camden (the fabulous Regina Fong, if anyone remembers) and once again was picked up by someone. Life was finally beginning!

I was ordained in March 1991 by Chief Rabbi Immanuel Jakobovits. At the ceremony, I was handed my certificate and another formal printed sheet in English and Hebrew, the terms and conditions. Nobody had told us about these beforehand, so they came as a surprise. Among the terms were clauses about 'moral turpitude' and about not 'sell[ing] yourself to a congregation of the ungodly' (that is, non-Orthodox). It was quite clear I was going to violate at least one of these. Later that year, I went to see my rabbi in Sydney to tell him about being gay. He was a hero of mine, and had stuck by me through my time in Israel, my flirtation with Catholicism and the rest. His first response was 'You can't be — you've gone out with my daughters!' He continued by saying that I could obviously not be a rabbi but that he would support me in finding academic work, though I should get married. It wasn't the best advice but I had really shocked him and I felt that probably no one had come out to him before, so he was struggling to find a response.

Meanwhile, I was struggling to accept an alternative to Orthodox Judaism as authentic. Then, in December of 1991, I read two books: *The Color Purple* by Alice Walker and a pioneering work of Jewish feminist theology called *Standing Again at Sinai* by Judith Plaskow. The effect of those two books together was to completely explode the patriarchal, judgemental image of God that I had been labouring under all those years. It showed me a much better (and to me a much truer) way of thinking about God — more loving, nurturing and affirming, much less hierarchical. It was a huge breakthrough for me, a moment where everything changed; it was quite marvellous. It also empowered me to make the decision that I had been avoiding and agonising about: to leave Orthodox Judaism and to seek some other way of being Jewish and a rabbi. Shortly after that in January 1992 I came out to Chief Rabbi Jonathan Sacks (who had been one of my teachers) and gave my notice in to the synagogue where I was working. Rabbi Sacks had called me in for a routine meeting, but I had come to tell him that I was leaving the United Synagogue and that I was homosexual (I still wasn't comfortable saying gay). He was visibly shocked and asked me if I was happy or unhappy in my homosexuality, and if I was sure. I told him that I was happy and sure. After pulling himself together, he told me why he believed Judaism is incompatible with homosexuality — arguments I knew already from reading his books, and disagreed with profoundly. He allowed me to serve out my six months' notice at Watford synagogue where I was working as long as I didn't cause a scandal — which was very decent of him. This period was very much about a feminist view of God and, although my personal journey was about being gay, it was all bound up with learning about the oppression of women, especially within Judaism. It was a personal revolution, in which I came to see the whole patriarchal structure of obedience in the Torah as harmful and damaging. I saw a better way.

After this, I began looking for a job. At first, I approached the Masorti movement, and was quickly informed that they weren't yet ready for a gay rabbi. All this time, I was becoming more and more involved in the Jewish Gay and Lesbian group and attended the first LGBT Jewish conference in London. There I was spotted by journalists, and the *Jewish Chronicle* began badgering me to come out. I didn't want to, of course, but there was a cool Jewish magazine at that time called *New Moon*. The magazine had been critical of Jonathan Sacks, especially of a charity walk that had taken place where all the Jewish charities had been encouraged to take part, but the Jewish Lesbian and Gay helpline had been turned down. Within the article on the charity walk, *New Moon* said, 'And we know of a young gay rabbi.' It was scary. The *Jewish Chronicle* told me that I would be outed and offered me an interview. Eventually, reluctantly, I caved in to the pressure and came out. I thought, 'That's the end of my chances of getting a job,' but out of the blue a job offer came from a small Liberal synagogue, not because I was gay but because of having been Orthodox. I was aware of Liberal Judaism, of course, but the idea that you could be Jewish via your father (rather than just your mother, as Orthodox Judaism says) was difficult for me to accept. However, then I met somebody who was a patrilineal Jew, a scholar and campaigner for the rights of other patrilineal Jews. Through talking to this new friend, I could identify my own suffering as a gay person with hers and became passionately convinced her cause was right. This made my transition to Liberal Judaism a lot easier. And that is how I made the change.

That feminist God kept me going and nurtured me for a number of years, but then came the third phase, around 2005 or 2006. At that point, I was feeling very angry about the homophobia within religious institutions: there was the bitter opposition to Civil Partnerships, there were homophobic stabbings at Jerusalem Pride, there was some nasty stuff within the Anglican Church and within Islam, and it was the heyday of Pope Benedict XVI in the Catholic Church. I was also having more and more doubts about the feminist, but still personal God I had believed in. Around that time, Richard Dawkins' book *The God Delusion* came out. I didn't read it at first, since I had seen all those arguments before, but then in early 2006 another book appeared, *The Dawkins Delusion?* by Alister McGrath. Being a fair-minded person, I thought I had better read the Dawkins book first. Although he doesn't really understand religion, the anger in his writing at the abuses perpetrated by religions struck a chord with me. Then I read *The Dawkins Delusion?* and found it pretty pathetic. I thought 'if this is the best religion can do, then religion really is in trouble.'

A key part of Dawkins' argument deals with the excommunicated 17th century Jewish philosopher Baruch Spinoza, which was significant for me as one of my fields of study and teaching has always been Medieval Jewish philosophy, a branch of thinking that partly culminates with Spinoza, whom I had so far avoided studying. Thanks to Dawkins I did start reading Spinoza, and there I found an idea of God that I felt dealt with a lot of the problems I was having at the time personally and intellectually — particularly on the problem of evil. For years and years, like most clergy of all religions, I had been facing questions about why God allows terrible things to happen. The traditional answers I gave people had stopped working for me. I became a convert to the idea of a completely impersonal God who does not will anything, who does not have any designs or plans, who is simply the creative force and energy within everything. It was a difficult transformation as this was very different from the traditional God of Jewish liturgy, but it was something I was determined to work on and have been working on ever since. I cautiously began talking about Spinoza, and even based a sermon for Yom Kippur (the Day of Atonement, the holiest day of the Jewish calendar) on his ideas. I was nervous about how people would react. Even though it was a Liberal synagogue, many people held a traditional theistic faith. Nonetheless, I was overwhelmed by the warmth of the reaction I received. At that point, Spinoza hadn't been talked about much within Liberal Judaism, so I began teaching more about this version of faith within the Liberal Jewish Synagogue (St John's Wood) and in Edinburgh. I found people were grappling with the same kinds of problems I was having, and yearning for answers. More recently, scholars like Rabbi Arthur Green in *Radical Judaism*, and the queer activist Jay Michaelson in *Everything is God*, have been moving in the same spiritual direction.

There have been challenges, of course. In the late 1990s, a huge controversy erupted in the Reform movement when the leading Reform Rabbi Elizabeth Tikvah Sarah gave a sermon one Yom Kippur that mentioned holding a 'Covenant of Love' ceremony for two women. This caused a huge furore in the Reform movement and threatened to split it, with large congregations threatening to secede. As part of the fallout from that, the Reform movement decided that every synagogue would hold a debate on these ceremonies. At that point there were only a handful of out rabbis, so I was asked to take part. The debates were truly horrible. The Reform movement had once been at the forefront of gay and lesbian acceptance in Judaism, but at this point the issue of commitment ceremonies proved explosive, and lots of unexpected, latent homophobia began pouring out. I was very involved, holding debates, organising petitions and so on. It was a tough time, but in the wake of this divisive, painful controversy, I decided to raise the issue within the Liberal movement at the annual rabbinic retreat. I was the only gay rabbi there, but I found a much more positive and relaxed response than within the Reform community. Not everybody was thrilled about the idea, but no threats or ultimatums were uttered. It was very comforting. My colleagues agreed to appoint a working group to discuss the issue, which allowed us to produce a comprehensive report and then produce a liturgy for same sex ceremonies, for which I was the editor. This took from about 2000 to 2004, at which point the government was bringing in Civil Partnerships, so by coincidence we dovetailed with the legal change. The Covenant of Love we published — the first from any Jewish movement in the world — was marriage in all but name, with the rituals and Hebrew terminology of marriage, even though we couldn't use the word 'marriage' itself in English. Later on, the Quakers, Unitarians and Liberal Judaism were the only three religious denominations campaigning wholeheartedly for equal marriage, which we were very proud of.

There are many other things to be proud of too. In the 1960s, Rabbi Lionel Blue and Rev Malcolm Johnson, the first out Anglican priest, started gay tea dances, and in the 1980s they went on to hold the first spiritual retreats for those with HIV/AIDS. This was a time when very little was being done for people of faith living with HIV. When I first came out, Lionel encouraged me to help lead the retreats in Somerset and London, which I did throughout the 1990s and into the early 2000s. In the early years, AIDS was still very often a terminal condition, so lots of people would be there who were seriously ill or dying. You would see people year after year, then they would disappear. HIV/AIDS was such a huge element of being gay throughout the 1980s and 1990s, and reclaiming that history, letting people know about it, is important. I am the custodian of a beautiful Jewish AIDS quilt, made by a friend of mine, an artist with HIV who was seriously ill (thankfully he survived). Unlike most of the quilts, which were made to remember one person, his was dedicated to all his friends who had died. It's embroidered with all the letters of the English and Hebrew alphabet, as well as pearls and sequins, a dove and a rainbow menorah (candelabrum). I bring it out for services every World AIDS Day. It's an important way of keeping those memories alive, as well as a vivid way of teaching about that history.

There is still further work to be done, of course. When we were working on our report for same-sex commitment ceremonies in the early 2000s, we were approached by a trans group asking to be included within the deliberations. At the time, we discussed it and decided it was too difficult. In retrospect, that is one of the moments I'm ashamed of. Though it was a collective decision, we missed the boat. Now, we are dealing with trans issues and I am proud to say that Liberal Judaism has been at the forefront of the movement, with projects called Rainbow Jews and Twilight People. Recently I have been rewriting our Hebrew marriage documents to be usable by non-binary and gender-fluid people. One of my former students has become the first trans rabbi in Britain. I do suspect we are still in the early stages and have much further to go in regard to gender and sexuality, but on the whole the Liberal movement has made a lot of progress since the late 1990s. So has the Reform movement, partly because of younger gay and lesbian rabbis, and partly because of the influence of Baroness Julia Neuberger, the Senior Rabbi of West London Synagogue, who has always been a bold advocate of gay rights.

This progress doesn't mean that every synagogue is inclusive, but things are improving all the time. As long as people face prejudice and struggle to come out, as lesbian or gay or bi or trans, we still have work to do. We're going in the right direction, but we aren't at the end of the journey.

Contributors

Séan Richardson is a writer, researcher, curator and podcaster based in Nottingham, a city he loves. The editor of *Unorthodox: LGBT+ Identity and Faith*, Séan has a history of working within queer and faith communities, and is currently finishing his PhD in queer literature and history.

Rev. Canon Dr Rachel Mann is an Anglican priest, poet and broadcaster. Author of seven books, her theological memoir of growing up trans, *Dazzling Darkness*, was a *Church Times* bestseller. Her latest book, *A Kingdom of Love* (Carcanet), is her debut full poetry collection.

Maryam Din is a queer Muslim activist, writer and speaker who co-founded the QTIPOC Notts group, organises vigils and protests and plays a major role with the LGBTQ community in Nottingham. Maryam has always been at the forefront of struggles for the recognition of QTIPOC people and fighting racism in the LGBTQ community and society. Living by a rule found in the Qur'an, 'to uphold justice and bear witness to God, even if it is against yourselves, your parents, or your close relatives' (An-Nisa, 4:135), Maryam can be found at the gym and working in equality, diversity and inclusion in the students' union sector.

Jaivant Patel is an award-winning dance artist, choreographer, cultural producer and artistic director of Jaivant Patel Dance. He is currently touring YAATRA, a captivating solo evening of Kathak and contemporary dance exploring the rich possibilities rooted in South Asian LGBTQ+ narratives. Jaivant is associate artist at Midlands Arts Centre and Arena Theatre.

As well as formidable accountancy experience and skills, **Isabella Segal** has something different to offer her clients — an incredible life story. Isabella is a General Practice accountant specialising in accounting, tax planning, business restructuring and recovery and complex tax enquiries. In May 2013 she transitioned to Isabella.

Sabah Choudrey is a reluctant activist on most things trans, brown and hairy. Co-founder of Trans Pride Brighton in 2013, and proud trans youth worker since 2014, forming Colours Network for BAME LGBTQ Youth Workers and Youth across the UK. Psychotherapist in training. Top three passions right now: carving out spaces for queer and trans people of colour, making friends with cats, and taking selfies from bad angles.

Selina Khunkhuna works for the NHS as a Service Manager and Cognitive Behavioural Psychotherapist. She supports people who suffer with anxiety and depression disorders. Selina has lived in Nottingham all her life, apart from when she studied in Manchester for four years.

Mr Ekow grew up in South London, surrounded by church, music and people. The result is a rapper, poet and producer using music to explore his internal and external world. Identifying as a British Ghanaian, Gay, Christian, his unique perspective lures listeners out of their comfort zones to become co-explorers.

Dr Siddhi Joshi is a marine biogeoscientist and LGBTI and human rights activist in Galway in Ireland. Brought up in South London, Siddhi founded the British Asian LGBTI online support group in 2013. She is a post-doctoral researcher in Geography in National University of Ireland Galway studying maerl habitats.

Khakan Qureshi is an LGBT+ campaigner, activist, writer and speaker shortlisted for several LGBT awards. Khakan organised the first South Asians LGBT Conference in 2018 in Birmingham and the first LGBTIQ+ Intersectionality and Islam Conference. He is the founder of Birmingham South Asians LGBT — Finding A Voice, a voluntary led, social support group for South Asian men and women, as well as a Stonewall LGBT School Role Model and Diversity Role Model.

Daljinder Johal works across journalism, marketing and production in addition to being a writer, publishing fiction and essays. She works with companies across the UK including ArtReach, LGBT+ organisation Gaysians, Heaux Noire, Beatfreeks and even makes worldwide connections with the literary journal, *Asymptote*. She's also part of Beatfreek's Youth Steering Committee, Graduates Unleashed's board and a board member at MAC Birmingham.

Ben and Robert have been a couple since meeting in 1971. Both are priests of the Church of England. Now retired, they remain active in the life of the Church in London, working in a number of different parishes and enjoying the fellowship of a wide range of people.

Rabbi Mark Solomon is minister of the Edinburgh and Leicester Liberal Jewish communities, senior lecturer in Rabbinic literature at Leo Baeck College, and Interfaith Consultant for Liberal Judaism. He was born in Sydney, and studied at Lubavitcher Yeshivot in Melbourne and Israel. He was ordained as an Orthodox rabbi at Jews' College, London, in 1991. After coming out — the first Orthodox rabbi to do so in Britain — he joined Liberal Judaism.

Acknowledgements

The stories contained within this book were drawn from oral history interviews conducted throughout the U.K. Those interviewed were found through existing connections, faith spaces, social media and word of mouth. Participants were able to opt for anonymity if they so wanted and were given the opportunity to edit their chapter before publication. Due to the diversity of opinion within this book, we have not attempted to explain religious terms or practices, as they mean different things to each contributor. We have also used a range of spellings, which reflect the participants' own use of different terms. It was a pleasure working with each and every contributor.

I am grateful to KeshetUK, Imaan, Sarbat, Liberal Judaism, British Asian LGBTI and everyone who helped to spread the word about this book. Thank you to all at Five Leaves, especially Ross and Myra for their generosity.

As ever, thank you to Jamie, Doug, Maya, Sarah, Sam, Dandie, Danny, Katie and Helen. To Richard. To Suzanne, Ian and Conor. You make me who I am.